MIXING TECHNIQUES

Printed by: MPG Books, Bodmin

Published by: Sanctuary Publishing Limited, Sanctuary House, 45-53 Sinclair Road, London
W14 0NS, United Kingdom. Web site: www.sanctuarypublishing.com

Copyright: Paul White, 2000
Sound On Sound web site: www.sospubs.co.uk

While the publishers have made every reasonable effort to trace the copyright owners for any or
all of the photographs in this book, there may be some omissions of credits for which we
apologise.

ISBN: 1-86074-283-1

basic
MIXING TECHNIQUES

PAUL WHITE

Also by Paul White from Sanctuary Publishing

Creative Recording I – Effects & Processors
Creative Recording II – Microphones, Acoustics,
   Soundproofing & Monitoring
Home Recording Made Easy
MIDI For The Technophobe
Live Sound For The Performing Musician
Recording & Production Techniques
Music Technology – A Survivor's Guide

Also in this series

basic DIGITAL RECORDING
basic EFFECTS AND PROCESSORS
basic HOME STUDIO DESIGN
basic LIVE SOUND
basic MASTERING
basic MICROPHONES
basic MIDI
basic MIXERS
basic MULTITRACKING

contents

chapter 3

chapter 4

chapter 5

introduction

The making of a high-quality record starts with a high-quality song, performance and recording, and the mixing process begins once all of the tracks have been recorded. A good mix can make a song really sparkle, while a poor one can make a brilliant musical performance sound like a cheap demo. There's no substitute for experience, but as demonstrated in the other books in this series, there are usually a few simple guidelines you can follow in order to obtain good results quickly; *basic MIXING TECHNIQUES* will help you to avoid making common mistakes and will provide you with a wealth of creative tips and tricks that will have you creating professional-sounding mixes in no time. It will also provide you with a glimpse into the world of post-production, including compiling albums, sweetening audio material, remixing and editing – the final steps in producing a professionally-recorded product.

Although the recording and engineering techniques discussed in this book are generally used by professionals, they can also be used in almost any type of home-recording situation, regardless of budget. In addition to my own experience, much of the information has been distilled from in-depth conversations with top producers and engineers across the world, and is applicable to a wide range of musical styles and disciplines.

planning

Although this books deals mainly with mixing, it's a fact that the success of your mix will depend largely on the quality of your original recording. If you're working on somebody else's material then you will have no control over this, but if you're carrying out your own recording as well as your own mixing you can make life a lot easier for yourself by taking care of some important details at the recording stage.

If you're working with other musicians, establishing a rapport with them is the first step towards gaining their confidence. Some will accept that they need the guidance of an experienced producer or engineer, while others will resent third-party interference. If you think the performance aspect could be handled more effectively but the artists think everything is fine then you will probably have to employ a little psychology rather than tell them outright that you don't think their current approach is working. An effective approach is to suggest something in such a way that the artists think that they thought of it themselves.

The first thing to do when planning a recording session is to listen to the artists' own demos, if they exist, so that you can get an idea of what the session will involve. The material may include the use of MIDI sequencing, in which case you'll need to have a copy of the relevant files so that you can verify that they're compatible with your system, and you'll also need to ensure that you have suitable MIDI instruments and samples to play back the various parts. Running a virus checker over any visiting disks is also a wise move, as not all clients are particularly hygienic when it comes to maintaining their software!

pre-planning MIDI

Even if the majority of the musical parts are to be sequenced at the mixing stage, it still helps to put a rough stereo mix of the sequenced backing onto tape so that the artists can then work on their overdubs without having to worry about loading sequences. Another reason for recording sequenced parts onto tape is that the available synths, drum machines and samplers might not have sufficient polyphony to cope with the entire performance in one take, and in this instance the sequence must be played through with some parts muted and the different sections must be recorded to tape in several passes. This might involve adding effects as the sounds are recorded onto tape, simply because several different instrumental or percussion sounds may have to share the same tape tracks. It's also important, whenever you make any edits, to save your work and to make regular backup disks.

vocals

The singer will often give his or her best performance when recording the guide track because there is less pressure to get it dead right, so it's important to record *everything*, even the level-checking run through. In most home-recording situations it's usual to record a vocal part all the way through and then run through it again, dropping in any phrases that weren't up to scratch. Some professionals work in this way as well, but they are more likely to record several complete takes on separate tracks, from which the producer will then compile one good-quality composite vocal track. The best phrases will be copied over onto to a new track, and if you have mixing automation or hard-disk editing equipment at your disposal then this is relatively straightforward, as long as you adopt an organised approach to your work. Whether you do the job manually or by using automation, keeping clear notes is essential in order to keep track of the wanted phrases during this process.

hardware

Although frivolous experimentation is a waste of time and money, it is well worth setting aside a little time to try out different mics and compressors as the vocalist warms up to find which give the best result. There are certain esoteric models known for their good vocal sound, but it's often found to be the case that a device that works magic for one singer may be quite unsuitable for another.

It's normal to apply a degree of compression to vocals, as they are recorded in order to obtain a healthy signal level that's reasonably even, but don't overdo things as excess compression is almost impossible to fix later – you can always add more compression during the mix, if you need to. Take the time to set up a good monitor mix for the singers, and ask them if they would like a little monitor reverb as this may help them to pitch their notes. Spill from the phones into the vocal mic is unlikely to be a problem except at very high monitoring levels or where a click track is involved, but if in any doubt then use fully-enclosed phones, as they leak less sound than the open-foam type. If you record everything without EQ it will make life easier when you come to mix, as it's not always possible to reverse the effects of EQ that has been applied during recording.

drums

If the session requires the use of a lot of real drums then you will find it worthwhile to read *basic MICROPHONES*, especially if you haven't worked with drums very often. The basic sound of the kit comes from the drums themselves rather than from the studio, so a well-maintained and well-tuned kit is essential. Rock drum sounds are usually recorded with the emphasis on the close mics, with overhead or ambient mics used to fill in the details, except on occasions when a very big, ambient drum sound is required, in which case a studio with a large live room should be used, with additional ambience mics placed at some distance from the kit.

Much modern pop music makes use of sequenced drum parts, which are often augmented by manual percussion, hi-hat and cymbal parts. This is an easy way to work because the basic drum rhythm is locked into the sequencer. If the session demands real drums all the way through, but some instruments are MIDI sequenced, then the drummer will have to play to a click track generated by the sequencer. The top session drummers can do this effortlessly, but other drummers may need some time to adapt to this manner of performing. Rather than deciding on either live or sequenced drums, consider the advantages of mixing both.

Sequencing the snare and bass drum avoids the problems snares rattling and toms booming whenever the bass drum is struck. As a rule, hi-hat and cymbal parts sound more natural when played live, especially if a 'human' feel is sought, although totally sequenced drum parts almost always work better for dance music, which is supposed to be more mechanical. Tom fills, ride cymbals and crash cymbals should also be played live if possible (provided that you're after an authentic sound) as they help considerably in lending a sequenced kick or snare track a sense of realism.

drum sounds

Pop music currently favours tight, solid bass-drum sounds, while dance music uses very bass-heavy, often synthesised sounds to create a relentless and powerful four-to-the-bar rhythm. Pop snare drums usually sound fairly natural, but there is still a lot of scope for variation depending on the style of song. Some pop songs demand a brighter, more jazzy snare sound, while for other songs a more techno sound is appropriate. If you're not sure which to use then try out a few contrasting styles, and keep an open mind when it comes to using something you may not have originally considered.

Dance snares tend to be light and bright and take back seat, while the bass drum provides the driving rhythm. These snare parts often play simple rhythmic figures rather than simply beating out two to the bar, and again composers of dance music usually sample drum sounds from other records, which are then further treated with effects or layered with other drum sounds. For those working without a sampler it is possible to trigger a bass-drum sound from a drum machine at the same time as a low-pitched burst of sound from a synthesiser to create a similar effect. Alternatively, the Simmons analogue electronic kick-drum sound is often emulated on modern drum machines, and this makes an ideal basis for a dance rhythm track. EQ can also be used to change existing sounds by a surprising degree, and the old trick of radically boosting the bass control while applying low mid cut at around 220Hz adds a lot of weight to the sound. The upper mid can be tuned to between 4kHz and 6kHz and boosted to produce a harder, more sharply-defined sound.

Traditional pop hi-hats tend to be fairly natural and bright, though the trend now is for pop music to draw on a wider range of influences, so there are no set rules. Many songs make effective use of the older analogue machine hi-hat sounds that are currently popular for dance, and numerous sample CDs are available that use processed non-musical sounds to create novel percussive elements, often with an industrial edge to them.

Suitable dance bass-drum sounds are to be found on many modern drum machines, but most inspiration can be obtained from the many dance records available. Hi-hat sounds are often either taken from the old Roland TR606 or 808 analogue drum machines or they are samples, filtered heavily to make them sound thin and artificial. Again, the of sample CD market provides plenty of variations.

rock drums

Despite its antiquity, heavy rock music refuses to go away! Rock kick drums are usually recorded with plenty of slap and a little after ring, while snares are quite deep with a well-defined sound. Like the bass drums the toms are recorded so that they sound quite solid, with a little ring and a nice sharp attack. The floor toms are usually tuned fairly deep, and there may be several higher-pitched toms, including smaller concert toms. Rock cymbal sounds are usually quite natural, with a fair selection of clanging cymbal 'bell' or 'earth ride' sounds. The hi-hats often have a fair amount of rattle, but this it acceptable and fits in well with the overall sound.

Traditional heavy rock rarely makes use of electronic drum sounds, and most drum machines contain a selection of suitable sampled 'real' sounds. The most important thing is to listen to how a real rock drummer plays and program the part accordingly as, while it is acceptable to use unnatural drum parts for dance music, rock drums require a sense of authenticity. In some situations sampled drum grooves may be more effective than programmed parts, unless you have a good drum programmer.

guitars

Guitar parts may be direct injected by using one of the studio pre-amps or speaker simulators currently available, though for heavy rock music the miked sound is still the preferred option. Chordal and rhythm parts can usually be DI'd very satisfactorily, while lead solos might benefit from the interaction between the amplifier and the guitar, especially if feedback is used to prolong sustained notes. Here you can mic up either a large stack or a small combo, though a large setup needs a large studio to produce the best results. A small combo produces excellent results in a small studio.

If two guitar parts need to be separated in some way, it can help to record one with a dynamic mic and the other with a capacitor mic. Further differences can be created by using humbucking or single-coil pickups, or with the subtle use of some effects such as chorus. Additionally, EQ can be used both on the amplifier and the mixing console to emphasise different parts of the audio spectrum, and of course the two parts can be panned to different sides of the stereo image when you come to mix.

Guitar treatments are covered in the mixing section of this book, but problems often arise when working with guitar bands when both guitar players want to play all of the time and they both want to play loud! If this is the case then return to the basic song and find out what it needs – not what the players' egos make them want to give it. Over-busy guitar parts are a problem often found with bands who play live on a regular basis but have little studio experience. The band will use a wall of sound to fill up their live sound, but in the studio the result is invariably far too cluttered.

Guitars with single-coil pickups take up less space in a mix yet will still cut through well, and that holds true for both clean and overdriven sounds. If two guitars need to play together, and both are using overdrive, then it's worth examining the musical lines to make sure that they aren't both playing the same thing for no good reason. Space can be created by making rhythm parts more rhythmic, rather than merely allowing one chord to sustain into the next, and it is often possible to reduce the amount of overdrive while recording, which will increase the amount of tonal shading present in the sound, even if it is compressed later. Indeed, overdrive is often used to create sustain, and it may be the case that a far more appropriate sound can be achieved by using less overdrive but combining it with compression.

It is possible to use the desk EQ to emphasise the 'bite' of the sound differently for each of the guitars in a mix. The presence or edge of a guitar can typically be anywhere between 2kHz and 6kHz, and by choosing a different frequency for each guitar and then boosting this by a few decibels the resulting sounds can be distanced even further. Additionally, if one guitar part is clearly the lead and the other plays more of a supporting role, a compressor or gate used in ducking mode can be used to punch the second guitar down by just 2-3dB while the lead guitar is playing. This small change in level have make a dramatic difference on the clarity of the mix, and the fact that the second guitar swells back in when the lead guitar stops will help to maintain the illusion of power and energy. This technique is something that should be tried at the mixing stage, when all parts have been safely recorded.

acoustic guitars

Acoustic guitars invariably sound better when miked up, regardless of how good the internal bug or pickup system may be, although some engineers use a mixture of the miked signal and the pickup to produce a pseudo-stereo effect. Important acoustic parts can be recorded in stereo, but in those cases when the guitar forms part of a complex arrangement a mono recording may well lend more stability. Because of the problems of leaking sound when working with acoustic instruments, acoustic guitars are usually overdubbed individually.

If a song starts with several bars of solo acoustic guitar, but you intend to record the acoustic guitar later as an overdub, it's important that the correct number of count-in bars is provided, indicated by a suitable click track or guide hi-hat part. If you ever have to pick up a project where one has not been provided, the easiest approach is to record the introduction separately and then edit the two sections together using a hard-disk editing system. If the two sections overlap you will need to use a multitrack hard-disk editing system.

problems?

A good producer/engineer will recognise the point at which an artist needs a break, so don't wear everyone out by endlessly repeating a part that clearly isn't working. Encouragement is important to singers and soloists, who can lose their confidence if things aren't going well. Take a break and try again later – recording that's fun to listen to is usually fun to make!

If you already have enough tracks to keep a previous take and can therefore allow the artist to perform another, the player may then feel relaxed enough to give a more flowing performance. The use of drugs and the excessive use of alcohol should obviously be discouraged, not only because of their detrimental effect on musical ability.

It's actually quite common for producers to edit together parts from several takes to provide one good version. For example, a one-off successful vocal chorus can be 'spun in' for each repetition of that section with a sampler, an open-reel stereo recorder or a tapeless multitrack system, while several imperfect guitar solos can often be edited to produce something acceptable.

arranging

When bands go to a studio to record they often assume that they can just do exactly as they do when playing live, but that's not always the best approach for making a quality recording. After all, the excitement and visual impact of a live performance often allows sections to be extended, but on a recording they could become boring. Here are a few quick tips that will help ensure that your song arrangement works.

The mechanics of musical arrangement can be divided into three basic areas: the order in which the various musical sections are presented (intro, verse, chorus, bridge, middle eight and so on), the musical lines and rhythms which make up each part, and the sounds chosen to play these lines and rhythms. The order in which the sections of a song are arranged is very important – commercial pop material tends to work to a fairly rigid formula in that a distinct intro is followed by between three and five minutes of music. The traditional, melodic pop song traditionally has an easily recognisable verse/chorus structure, usually with a middle eight (which, despite its name, doesn't need to be exactly eight bars long), one or two bridge sections, and an instrumental solo (although this is not obligatory).

The chorus will be repeated frequently, and songs are often faded out over a repeated chorus line. Although musical fashions change very quickly, this traditional song structure has proved to be something of a survivor. Having said that, if you're putting together a dance song, you'll probably be more concerned by its dynamics – the way in which the songs builds and then drops back – than by conventional structure.

Because of the nature of the commercial music market, a song has to attract the interest of the listener very quickly. Once the intro is over, it usually pays to get to the chorus pretty quickly. This may be achieved in a number of ways, for example by shortening the first verse, by using a modified version of the chorus as an intro, or coming straight in with the chorus after the intro.

Another useful trick is to use only part of the chorus when it first occurs, as this creates a sense of anticipation, helping to keep the listener interested, even if they've heard the song a few times. The ability to create an atmosphere of anticipation is the hallmark of a good songwriter, and often the ends of verses or link sections will contain musical hooks that make the listener want to keep listening until the chorus.

A good hook can be anything memorable, from a brass riff or a drum fill to a vocal phrase or synthesiser line. The important thing is that it's catchy and easily identifiable. It's also helpful if the verse contains a hook of some sort, but again this can be created by the clever use of melody, by repetition or simply by the distinctive vocal character of the singer. If you're trying to create a track for the pop market then don't feel that you're above using something that sounds childish or musically immature – the majority of singles buyers are not noted for their appreciation of the finer points of musical construction, so if it works then use it!

As mentioned earlier, dance tracks tend to have little formal structure, although they do tend to obey their own rules, despite their apparent intent to be non-conformist. Even so, most successful dance records combine a compelling rhythm with a series of musical hooks to make the result more appealing and to help it stand out from the competition. The musical tempo of most such records is quite predictable and lies within fairly rigidly-defined limits for each style, but it's possible to superimpose other rhythmic patterns on top of the straight four-to-the-bar rhythm to make the piece more interesting as a whole. In this respect there is no substitute for analysing existing music to find out exactly what makes it tick. Most good pop songs are fairly easy to analyse, as there is usually not much going on at any one time. If anything, American pop arrangements are musically more busy than British songs, but it's interesting to note that many of the instruments are kept very low in the mix, especially distorted guitars, with the vocal line right up in the front of the mix.

It always pays to analyse successful singles to find out how they work. See if you can identify the hooks in a song and hear how they work. While you shouldn't aim to copy another track there is no substitute for analysing existing music to absorb song construction and arrangement tricks of the trade.

more on arrangement

At the heart of virtually every pop song is the rhythm section, which might take the form of traditional drums and bass or may be entirely electronic, using drum machines and synthesisers. Either way, the idea is to make the bass instrument and the underlying drum rhythm work together to establish the rhythm, feel and groove of the piece. The way in which this is done depends on the type of music with which you are working, as there are definite styles and rules which exist for specific musical forms (funk, reggae, dance and so on), and these are quite evident after listening to a few records in each genre. Even though the approach of these styles may be quite different, they all share a similar approach in that the bass and drums work together as a unit and not as independent entities.

- Guitars and vocals usually occupy the mid ground of the musical frequency spectrum, as do pad keyboard parts, so it's important that none of these parts conflict. Where there is a danger of the sound becoming muddled, parts can be separated to some degree by changing the basic sounds and making them thinner, for example by removing some low mid when mixing with EQ, by emphasising different parts of the upper mid by subtly using EQ boost, and by panning. However, don't rely on panning to solve all of your problems as it's still important for a mix to sound good in mono. If the problem persists, re-examine the musical arrangement and question the role of each sound or musical line you've chosen. Every part should exist for a reason, and if you discover one that has no reason to be there then you're probably better off leaving it out.

- The bright synth sounds – cymbals, acoustic guitars, high percussion and so on – lie at the top of the audio spectrum, and these add detail and interest to a mix that might otherwise be bass and mid heavy. Bright sounds needn't be loud in order to provide the necessary musical punctuation, and if high-pitched synth lines or high percussion parts are planned then it may be wise to examine any cymbal or hi-hat parts to avoid overcrowding.

- Pad keyboard parts can either be placed low in the mix or they can filtered so that they occupy a narrower part of the audio spectrum. Beware of pad sounds that muddy the low end.

- Synthesised sounds can be corrected at source, while organ sounds can be set up by using the drawbars and then filtered with EQ. For example, it might be useful to roll off all frequencies below 150Hz to thin out the sound, as this will help avoid potential muddiness in the vulnerable lower mid part of the audio spectrum.

- Riffs played on instruments such as brass don't usually present a problem, as they are usually used strategically rather than simply allowed to play throughout the piece. Guitar riffs, on the other hand, are often allowed to continue over verses or choruses. Clean guitar sounds tend to be easier to integrate into a mix than heavily distorted sounds, hence the popularity of using bright guitar riffs to underpin soul music, and a bright chordal sound cuts through well in any mix without killing other sounds that occur at the same time.

Once all of the necessary parts are recorded to the best of your ability, the monitor mix you've been setting up as the recording progresses should give you a good idea of how the final mix will sound. However, unless time is really tight, the mix proper should be done on a different day so that you can hear it with fresh ears. Loud sounds affect the way in which we perceive sound, so it's important to let your ears and your mind rest.

mixing tools

Mixing requires an accurate monitoring system set up in an appropriate room, a good-quality mixer with enough channels to handle all of the signals that need to be mixed, and certain signal-processing devices such as reverb units, compressors and multi-effects units.

monitor speakers

An accurate pair of monitor speakers is essential when mixing to hear exactly how a mix sounds. A theoretically perfect speaker would reproduce the entire audio spectrum with no distortion or coloration, but because of the limitations of both physics and expenditure there are inevitably compromises that must be made.

Near-field monitors are popular in both professional and home studios. These are small but nominally accurate loudspeakers that can be used close to the listening position, thus minimising any undesirable effects from the acoustics of the room. The closer you are to the speakers the greater the proportion of direct sound you hear, compared with the sound reflected from the room. Also, the closer you sit to a speaker the less power you need to produce an adequate monitoring level.

Small hi-fi speakers are often suitable, as long as they are selected for honest sound reproduction rather than an ability to flatter the music. Don't expect to get deep bass from small speakers, however – in reality a very deep bass response is undesirable because the results will be unpredictable, unless the room is acoustically designed to handle it, leading to inaccurate mixes that don't sound right on other audio systems.

A good two-way loudspeaker system with a bass driver of between five and eight inches in diameter is usually more than adequate for home studio use, especially when used in the near field. This may be powered from a hi-fi amplifier, but don't skimp on power or your system might not be able to handle peaks such as drum beats cleanly. Around 50 watts per channel should be considered a realistic minimum, even if monitoring at moderate levels.

where to mix?

Domestic living rooms and bedrooms absorb quite a lot of sound because of the amount of carpeting, curtains and soft furnishings usually present, but because we're used to listening to music under these conditions a studio with a similar acoustic characteristic makes a perfectly workable alternative to a purpose-built studio. Because no monitoring systems or rooms sound exactly alike it's important to compare mixes with commercial music played back over the same system in the same room. Bedrooms or other domestic rooms with carpets and soft furnishings are perfectly adequate for mixing music demos and even some commercial projects. If the room seems too lively or reverberant, hanging rugs or heavy curtains on the rear wall and at either side of the mixing position often helps.

speaker positions

Speakers should be arranged so that they form two points of an equilateral triangle, with the listener at the apex, sitting at the mixing console. They should be angled inward so that they point directly at the listener's head, and they should be at around head height. You should avoid putting speakers in or close to corners, as this has an unpredictable effect on the sound of the bass end. You may seem to get more bass by doing this, but in reality you'll probably EQ your mix to compensate for it so that, when you play your songs back on another system, they'll sound bass light. Figure 2.1 shows the position of the monitor speakers relative to the listener.

effects

Whereas conventional instruments are usually played in real acoustic spaces to give them character, electronic instruments, or 'acoustic' sounds recorded in an acoustically 'dead' studio, usually rely on electronic effects to make them sound real and interesting. In today's MIDI studio many instruments, modules and

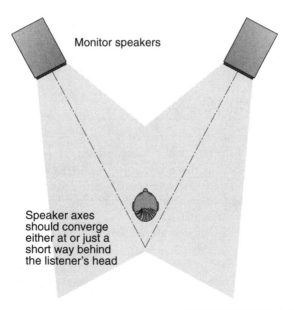

Monitor speakers

Speaker axes should converge either at or just a short way behind the listener's head

Figure 2.1: Monitor positions

soundcards come with their own effects, though if these are inadequate in any way then external effects may also be connected via a mixer. There are also software-based effects available, such as the VST plug-ins used with the leading MIDI-plus-audio sequencer. The basic principle is the same wherever your effects originate, however, and the next few pages describe the more common effects and their applications.

reverberation

Most contemporary music is performed indoors, where a degree of room reverberation is expected. Conversely, much pop music is recorded in relatively small, dry-sounding studios, so artificial reverberation has to be added in order to create a sense of space and realism. Reverberation is created naturally when a sound is reflected and re-reflected from the surfaces within a room, hall or other large structure.

Before digital reverb units were introduced, live echo rooms, spring reverb units and echo plates were all used to add reverberation to recordings. The reverb plate comprised a large steel plate suspended in a rigid frame and driven into vibration by a voice coil similar to that on a loudspeaker. The resulting vibrations were picked up by two or more surface-mounted contact mics and

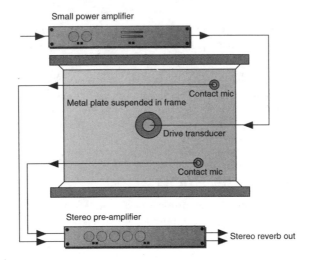

Small power amplifier

Contact mic

Metal plate suspended in frame

Drive transducer

Contact mic

Stereo pre-amplifier

Stereo reverb out

Figure 2.2: Plate reverb

amplified before being fed back into the mix. The final effect was brighter than natural reverb, but it was a musically pleasant sound, which is why most modern digital units have plate simulation modes as well as those which simulate the reverb found in rooms, halls and chambers. Figure 2.2 illustrates how plate reverb works.

Digital reverberation units simulate this natural phenomenon by creating thousands of random echoes every second, and most provide a choice of treatments, from small rooms to great echoing caverns. Though long reverb times are initially impressive, most musical applications require a relatively short reverb time of under two seconds, where the reverb time is defined as the time taken for the reverb to die down by 60dB relative to its initial level. Figure 2.3 describes the main stages of reverberant decay.

A popular digital reverb setting is the plate, which is a patch designed to simulate mechanical plate reverbs. The plate setting has a bright, diffuse sound that works well on virtually anything, from drums to vocals.

Electronic reverb devices produce a stereo output, which is how they create the illusion of spaciousness, even though the sound that is treated may be in mono. The reverb unit's outputs should be panned hard left and right to obtain a natural result, regardless of where the original, dry signal is panned in the mix. This will happen automatically if the effects are plugged into the stereo returns of a mixer, and if the effects are internal to a soundcard or module then the added effects will be also be heard in stereo.

On an artistic level, busy music works best with shorter reverb settings while slower, less complicated music can benefit from longer settings. It can help to avoid putting much reverb on bass sounds, if any, as this can make the mix sound muddy. Listen to other records to hear how reverb has been used on them. You'll probably be surprised at how little is required to achieve the desired result.

echo and delay

Echo was used extensively on both guitars and vocals in the Sixties and Seventies, though at the time it was created with a tape loop rather than digital electronics. Unlike reverb, delay produces distinct, evenly-spaced repeats, and multiple decaying echoes can be created by feeding some of the output back into the input

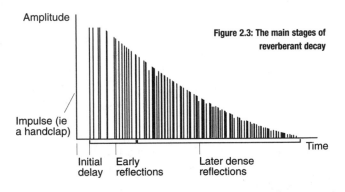

Figure 2.3: The main stages of reverberant decay

(there is a control for this). If you set the delay time to a multiple of the tempo of the song then some very interesting rhythmic effects can be created. Try delay on drums as well as vocals, guitars and keyboard sounds. Numerous variations on delay are available, such as multitapped delay, with which two or more echoes are generated at once, each with different delay times. There are also 'ping pong' delays, which cause the echoes apparently to bounce from side to side.

chorus and flanging

Chorus is based on a short delay combined with pitch modulation to create the effect of two or more instruments playing the same part. The original (dry) part is accompanied by a slightly delayed part that fluctuates slightly in pitch, thus creating the illusion of the presence of an ensemble.

Flanging is also a modulated delay effect, but the delay time is very short and feedback is used to create a much stronger effect, not unlike the old trick of tape phasing. Both of these treatments work well on synth pad sounds, such as strings, and are best used in stereo, where they create a sense of movement as well as width. Because flanging is quite a dramatic effect, it is best used sparingly.

pitch shifters

Pitch shifters are found in almost all external multi-effects units, though they are usually not included in soundcards. Furthermore, when you're working purely with MIDI sounds you can change pitch simply by transposing a part.

As the name implies, pitch shifters can change the pitch of an original audio signal, usually by up to an octave in either direction. Small pitch shifts are useful for creating detuning or doubling effects (a nice alterative to chorus), while shifts of whole semitones can be used to create octaves or parallel harmonies.

using effects

Electronic effects such as those described have become an integral part of modern music recording, but it's wrong to think of an effect as something that is added at the last minute to provide a kind of superficial gloss. It's also wrong to assume that using an effect will cover up a mistake or a piece of poor playing because, in most instances, it will simply draw attention to it. Though the experienced engineer may use effects in apparently unconventional ways, the less experienced musician may find the following notes helpful.

Reverberation is probably the most important of all studio effects as it needs to be added to most recordings in order to simulate a natural acoustic environment. All other effects are employed for artistic reasons, and, although reverb can be used artistically, it's main purpose is to create a sense of realism and dimension.

It helps to plan very early on in a mixing session the type of effect that will be used. Some effects play an integral role in the sounds used in a composition, while certain delay-based effects may help define the rhythm of a piece of music. In the studio the producer has to decide which effects need to be added during the recording stage, if any, and which can be left until the mix. The home recorder faces the same decisions, though some of them may be determined by the number of recording tracks and effects units available.

recording with effects

Though leaving all effects until the mix will allow more room to manoeuvre, this is not always the best way to work, even if the facilities exist to make this practical. Sometimes it helps to record an effect to tape with the original instrument. A good engineer or producer will know instinctively when an effect should be added during recording and when it should be left until the mix. Indeed, the open-ended way of leaving everything to the mix can have a detrimental effect on the production of a piece of music: I've spoken to several producers who believe that it's a good idea to commit to something fairly rigid at an early stage, as failure to do so can lead to a huge amount of time wasted in exploring different possibilities when all that was needed was a clear sense of direction in the beginning. To make matters more complicated we now have MIDI sequencers synchronised to tape or hard disk, multitrack machines, mix automation and hard-disk digital editing. All of these technological developments, while wonderful and extremely useful in themselves, can divert much time and effort from the task of making good music. Clarity of purpose when mixing is therefore essential, especially if your studio time is limited.

when to add effects?

It's important to consider both the artistic and logistic implications of either recording effects to multitrack or saving them until the mix. There are two main factors in favour of recording the effect along with the original instrument: firstly, the player may feel more comfortable using effects and so give a better performance (though it is possible to add effects to the headphone monitor mix without actually recording them); secondly, committing effects when recording saves time at the mixing stage. It also frees up the effects unit in question for a different task later in the session – for example, a multi-effects unit could provide an echo or delay during recording and then be used to add reverb during mixdown.

Conversely, if effects are changed or left out at the recording stage, the original musical performances may no longer work effectively. This is very often the case when delay effects are used, as the musician plays to the effect, but it can apply equally to the chorus-type treatments often used on guitar parts.

There also are negative aspects to recording with effects, however, especially if the number of tracks is limited, as it might be with a small analogue or MiniDisc recorder. Recording an instrument in mono only takes one track, but if you want to add a stereo effect you'll need to use up two tracks in order to keep the effect in stereo. You could stick with one track if you have a limited number of tracks available, but that would leave the effect in mono.

Committing effects to tape also deprives you of the opportunity to fine-tune the effect later on, to change its pan position relative to the dry track and to change its level in the mix.

There are occasions when one or the other approach is more appropriate, and it's unwise to develop a method of working which is too rigid and deprive yourself of flexibility. If time is limited then recording as many effects as possible while tracking certainly saves time during mixing.

guitar effects

Guitar parts are usually recorded with their basic effects, including overdrive, spring reverb and expressive pedal effects such as wah wah. Some analogue effects pedals produce a more musical sound than their better-specified rack-mounted counterparts, especially chorus and flange units, while stereo reverb treatments can safely be left to the final mix. Don't be tempted to dismiss an effects pedal purely because of its technical specification – if it sounds good then use it. If it's too noisy, or if it distorts or causes some other problem, have a word with the player using it and see if you can simulate the sound with your own equipment. Even if you decide to add the effect in the final mix you should still be able to arrange things so that the player can monitor his part with his own effect while recording. This can usually be achieved by feeding the effect to the monitor mix without recording it.

If it proves necessary to leave a guitar treatment open ended, it may help to record the sound required by the player on one track and a straight, clean, DI'd output from the guitar on a spare track via a DI box. In this way it's possible to feed the dry guitar track through an amplifier/recording pre-amp with the desired effects and overdrive settings if the original recording isn't as good as you'd hoped. This is easily achieved by playing the DI'd guitar back through an amp, miking up the amp in the normal way and then recording the sound onto a new track.

logistics

In some circumstances it's necessary to record effects with the performance purely because there aren't enough effects units or console sends to go around when mixing. Similarly, if tracks have to be bounced in order to free up space, the necessary effects must be added during the bounce. If track restrictions mean that the bounced signal ends up on a single track then any added effects will also be in mono. This is a common problem in smaller home studios, and the usual outcome is that many of the effects which should have been in stereo end up being in mono. There is no easy way around this, but it is possible to achieve some semblance of a stereo spread on a mono track by processing it at the final mixing stage with an additional stereo reverb treatment. If the track needs little in the way of added reverb then a short, bright plate or an early reflection/ambience program will create a sense of depth and width without making the sound seem as though extra reverb has been added.

If your main restriction is in the number of console sends available then you should consider using the channel insert points or direct outputs as sends when adding effects to individual tracks. If you have sufficient spare input channels on the mixer then you can use these as effects returns so that you can then make use of the EQ and pan controls. Ensure that the effects sends are turned down on any channels used as returns, however, or you may end up with unwanted feedback.

innovative effects

While most effects can be generated by using either dedicated effects units, digital multi-effects processors or software effects plug-ins, it is possible to create something a little out of the ordinary by using nothing more than a little ingenuity. Many of the recordings still regarded as pop classics were made in the days when very few effects units were available and engineers had to improvise.

Some of the most powerful effects are the most simple to create, and one of my favourites is true backwards reverb. This is quite unlike the canned reverse effects that come as standard on most reverb units, in that it actually comes before the sound that caused it. Obviously this can't be achieved in real life, and it can't be done in real time, either, because the reverb unit would have to know what sound was coming next. Nevertheless, it can be done on tape and is relatively straightforward. If you're working with analogue tape, follow these steps and try the effect for yourself.

- Record the original take dry onto the multitrack tape and then turn the tape over so that the track plays backwards, from the end of the song to the start. (Turning the tape over also reverses the track order so that, on an eight-track machine, track one becomes track eight and vice versa, so make sure that you don't record over any wanted material while the tape is reversed.)

- With the recording now running backwards the track to be treated is fed through a conventional stereo reverb unit set to a medium-to-long decay setting (two to ten seconds) and the reverb recorded onto an empty track, or a pair of tracks if you can afford the luxury of keeping it in stereo.

- Once the reverb has been recorded the tape can then be switched back the right way round and played normally. Now the reverb will start to build up a couple of seconds before the track starts and produce an unnatural pre-echo effect. This works very nicely on vocals and can also be used on instrumental sounds, including drums.

- Panning the dry sound to one side of the mix and the reverse reverb to the other creates a strong sense of movement, and it's worth experimenting with combining effects, such as adding artificial reverse reverb to the track at the same time and panning this to the other extreme.

Unfortunately this practise is impossible on a digital tape machine, but if you have a computer audio system then the chances are that there will be a facility that allows you to reverse sections of the audio files which you have recorded. In this case you can simply reverse the section you want to process, add reverb using a software plug-in or an external processor, and then record the result to another track. Finally, you can reverse the processed track again so that it plays the right way round once more. Now what you'll hear is the reverb building up first, followed by the original dry sound.

pitched reverb

A reverb unit will normally be fed directly from the track being treated, but there are a couple of tricks that can be used to make the effect more interesting. One is to feed the effects send through a pitch shifter before it goes to the reverb unit and either raise or drop the pitch by an octave. This means that the original sound will be unchanged but its reverb will be an octave lower (or higher) than normal. If used on musical sounds the shift in pitch must be either a whole octave up or down in order to maintain a true musical relationship, but with drums and other percussion smaller shifts can be used.

reverb and flange

Flanging is a very dramatic effect, which means that it can be too obvious if used normally. However, if you patch in a flanger between the desk's aux send output and the input to the reverb unit, the result is far more subtle than that achieved by putting the flanger after the reverb output, and it helps to add sparkle and interest to both vocal and instrumental sounds. This technique works nicely with synthesised string sounds as the flanger creates a sense of detail and movement in the reverberant sound, and the fact that the flanger is positioned before the reverb rather than after it means that the cyclic nature of the effect is disguised by the multiple delays of the reverb unit.

real shift

Pitch shifters can be used to thicken a vocal or instrumental track by providing a slightly detuned version of the original, but unless you have a really good pitch shifter the processed sound may not be as clear as the original. If you've come across this problem before then you could try the following technique, which allows you to use any old pitch shifter and still produces master-quality results.

The idea is a variation on the old trick of doubling an original vocal part by singing along to the original. The difference is that this time the signal feeding the singer's headphone monitor system is processed through the pitch shifter so that it is between five and ten cents sharp or flat.

The singer then pitches his or her performance to the shifted sound, with the result that the new take is shifted a few cents away from the original – exactly the right amount to create a natural chorus effect. If you haven't run out of tracks then try the same thing again on a new track, but this time with the pitch shifted in the opposite direction. This will produce triple tracking, in which the two new parts are pitched to an equal degree on either side of the original.

If the pitch shifter has a delay function then a delay of a few tens of a millisecond can be added in order to shift the second take slightly in time as well as pitch. The advantage here (as well as having a real instead of synthesised second take) is that the quality of the delay unit or pitch shifter is totally irrelevant, as the shifted sound is used only for monitoring and not for recording.

There is no need even to use a pitch shifter to monitor instruments; all that you need to do is change the recorder speed slightly (with the varispeed control if you're using a tape machine) and then record a second take without retuning the instrument. When the tape is replayed at the normal speed the two slightly out-of-tune takes will produce a much more natural chorus effect than that obtained with the use of any chorus pedal.

effects and processors

This section is very important, and understanding its implications will mean avoiding a lot of trouble and frustration when connecting effects and processors. First, however, a definition: the term 'effects' is used here to describe those devices that rely on some form of delay circuitry for their operation, while the term 'processor' describes any type of outboard device that processes the entire signal, changing it either tonally or in level.

While it is permissible to connect any type of effect or signal processor via a mixer insert point, there are limits to what can be used via the aux send/return system. As a rule of thumb, only delay-based effects – such as reverb, echo, chorus, phasing, flanging and pitch shifting – should be connected via the aux system, and these are generally grouped under the term 'effects'. If the box uses delay, or if there's a dry/effect mix knob or parameter, then it's almost certain to be an effect. Effects are unique in that they aren't added to the original signal. A process, such as EQ, doesn't add to the original signal but instead changes it. Processors include compressors, gates and equalisers, which may only normally be connected via insert points, not via aux sends and returns. There are workarounds to specific problems that may involve connecting processors to the aux send system but these procedures fall outside their normal usage.

If insert points are used to connect effects then the dry/effect balance must be set at the effects unit.

compressor/limiters

Compressors are used to even out the excessive peaks in signal level that occur in vocal or instrumental performances by changing the gain of the signal path in relation to the level of the signal passing through. Just as an engineer might pull down a fader if the level gets too high, so a compressor will turn down the level if it exceeds a threshold set by the user. Signals falling below the threshold level remain unchanged. The degree of gain reduction which is applied is set by the compression ratio control setting, as shown in the graph in Figure 2.4.

When the ratio is very high, the compressor's maximum output is maintained at the threshold level and is effectively prevented from going beyond it. This sets a limit on the maximum signal level regardless of the input, and a compressor used with a high ratio setting is often described as a limiter, hence the term compressor/limiter. As a rule, high compression ratios are used in conjunction with high threshold settings so that only the signal peaks are affected. Lower ratios may be used with lower threshold settings to provide gain levelling over a greater dynamic range.

The compressor's attack control determines how quickly the circuitry responds once a signal has exceeded the threshold, while the release control sets the time for the gain to return to normal once the input has dropped back below the threshold. Some compressors have auto attack and release settings that respond to the dynamic character of the input signal.

Figure 2.4: Compressor ratio graph

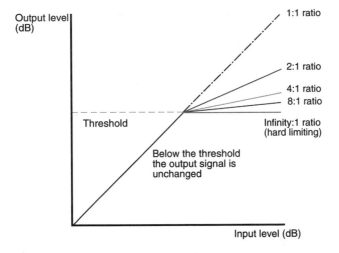

Auto mode is very useful for processing signals with constantly-changing characteristics, such as vocals, slap/pull bass guitar and complete mixes.

Most two-channel compressors have a Stereo Link switch, and if this is thrown then stereo signals can be processed. In Link mode both channels are compressed by the same amount, thus preventing the image from moving to one side or the other when a loud sound appears on only one side of the mix.

The maximum gain of a compressor occurs when the input signal falls below the threshold, which can sometimes lead to the boosting of background noise during quiet passages or pauses. To combat this problem some compressors are equipped with built-in gates which silence the signal during pauses.

Compressors are most often used to keep instruments and vocals at an even volume during a mix, although they may also be used to add sustain to guitars. Setting a deliberately long attack time can also help to emphasise the attack of a sound such as the slap of the bass guitar.

Limiting is used in those circumstances when it would be undesirable for a signal to exceed a specific level (to prevent clipping on a digital recorder, for example).

gates

Whereas compressors control the levels of signals that exceed a threshold, gates control the levels of signals that fall below a threshold. Their purpose is to silence the signal during pauses, when any background noise will not be masked by the presence of a signal. If the threshold level is set just above the background noise then the gate will operate whenever there is a pause in the signal.

Gates are used for muting spill from other instruments as well as for tackling straightforward noise or hiss problems, and they are regularly used when miking drum kits to prevent the bass drum mic from picking up the other drums in the kit, for example. They are also used with electric guitars to combat the high level of noise and hum generated by a typical guitar amplifier when the guitarist is not actually playing. Vocals may also be gated to hide the sounds of rustling clothing or breathing.

It must be understood that gates only remove noise when there is a pause in the wanted signal – they can't help with noise that is audible over the top of the programme material. Even so, using gates on all of the noisy tracks in a multitrack recording can help produce a much cleaner-sounding recording. Figure 8.5 shows a gate's reaction when the signal falls below the threshold level. Expanders are very similar to gates, although they close down gently, rather like a compressor in reverse.

equalisers

Equalisers are essentially tone controls, and there are a number of varieties. Most mixers have built-in EQ, but it's often useful to have a better-quality external equaliser that can be patched in via an insert point for those occasions when more precise control is required. Parametric equalisers are the most versatile, but they also take the longest amount of time to set up properly.

exciters

Also known as enhancers, exciters are devices that add synthesised high-frequency harmonics to a signal to make it sound brighter and more intimate than it did originally. The process was developed and patented by the company Aphex and is different to equalisation, which can only redistribute the harmonics that already exist. Exciters are used to push sounds to the front of the mix and to create clarity and space in crowded mixes. They can be used on whole mixes or just on individual tracks, and they may also be used to brighten stereo mixes destined for masters and mass cassette copying in order to help compensate for the loss of high-frequency content that cassette duplication inevitably entails.

Enhancers working on slightly different principles are available from other manufacturers.

autopanners

An autopanner is simply a device that automatically pans a mono signal from left to right in the mix, usually under the control of a low-frequency oscillator or external trigger, and can be quite subtle if used in time with the tempo of a track. Many multi-effects units include a panning facility as well as a rotary speaker emulator, which is a setting designed to simulate Leslie speakers, along with similar systems that employ rotating baffles to add vibrato to organ sounds. Most rotary speaker sounds combine panning with chorus, and they often have two speeds with a delayed accelerate and decelerate function to mimic the mechanical inertia of the real thing.

patching

Patching effects and processors can be confusing, so I've included this list of key points for reference.

- Insert points are invariably presented as stereo jacks wired to carry both the send and return signal, so if you don't have a patchbay you'll need a Y-lead with a stereo jack on one end and two monos on the other.

• Processors must always be used in line with a signal and not in the effects send/return loop unless you're sure about exactly what you are doing and why you're doing it.

• Most processors work at line level, so you can't plug a mic directly into them. The correct way to compress a mic signal, for example, is to patch the compressor into the insert point of the mic channel, as the mixer's mic amp will then bring up the mic signal to line level before feeding it to the compressor.

• If an effect is used via the aux/send return system it is normal to set the effects unit's dry/effect balance to effect only, so that the console's aux send controls can then determine the effect balance.

• Some effects, such as phasing and flanging, rely on a precise effect/dry balance which may be better accomplished in the effects unit itself. In this case, you should patch the effects unit into an insert point. If you must use the aux/send system, you should either de-route the channel from the stereo mix to kill the dry signal or feed the effects unit from a pre-fade (foldback) send and turn down the channel fader.

• To use a mono in/stereo out effects unit (such as

reverb or stereo delay) via insert points, simply route one output of the unit to the insert return of the channel feeding it and the other to the insert return of an adjacent channel. Match the levels, and pan one track hard left and the other hard right for maximum stereo effect.

• To use a stereo in/stereo out effects unit via insert points, use two adjacent mixer channels panned hard left and right.

• To treat a whole mix with EQ or compression, for example, patch your processor into the master insert points. This places your unit in the signal path just before the master stereo faders, which means that, if you're using a compressor, it won't try to fight you if you perform a fadeout. Similarly, any noise generated by the processor will also be faded as you pull the faders down.

• If you don't have master insert points you can patch a processor between the mixer's stereo out and the input to your stereo mastering recorder. However, if you want to perform fades with a compressor patched in, you'll need to use the input level control on the tape machine rather than on the desk.

recording vocals

Vocals, it can be argued, are the most important part of any mix, which is why I'm devoting an entire chapter to the subject. It's essential to start with a high-quality recording, but even if you don't have any particularly esoteric equipment you can still acquire a reasonable basic sound by using a good dynamic or capacitor mic in conjunction with a pop shield and recording with no EQ or other effects. If you have a good compressor then by all means compress slightly when recording. Use blankets to deaden room reflections, if necessary, and maintain a distance of six to twelve inches between the singer and the mic, as shown in Figure 3.1. Also, it's important to pay particular attention to deadening the area behind the singer, as sound can reflect from hard surfaces back into the mic. Further tips on recording vocals are detailed at the end of this chapter, and the subject is covered in depth in the book on *basic MICROPHONES*, also in this series.

Once you have recorded a good vocal part you will invariably need to employ a suitable reverb or ambience

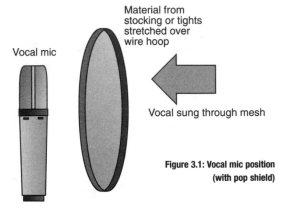

Vocal mic

Material from
stocking or tights
stretched over
wire hoop

Vocal sung through mesh

Figure 3.1: Vocal mic position
(with pop shield)

Mic distance between 6 and 12 inches from mouth

treatment in order to add realism, especially if the vocals were recorded in a dead-sounding studio. Furthermore, some degree of additional vocal compression is usually necessary, even if some was added during recording. Compression also helps to guard against volume peaks that might otherwise cause distortion due to the tape overloading. Soft-knee compressors are the least obtrusive in this application, and should be set to provide a gain reduction of 10dB or so during the louder sections. If you're recording a singer with a very wide dynamic range, on the other hand, you may need a ratio-type controller set to a ratio of 4:1, or even higher, in order to keep the peaks under control. Choose a fast or programme-dependent attack time and a release time of around half a second as a starting point.

Because adding too much compression at the tracking stage may ruin an otherwise perfect recording, the majority of engineers will use additional compression when mixing rather than try to judge the exact amount when recording. However, you should be aware that the use of compression also brings out any noise and sibilance already present in the recording. Using an exciter, high-end EQ or a bright reverb setting to add presence to a vocal track may also bring out sibilance to an unacceptable level, in which case it may prove necessary to use a de-esser when it comes to mixing in order to keep the sibilance under control. If you do end up using a de-esser, you must ensure that it is connected via the console's insert points.

A gate or expander can prove useful in cleaning up the spaces between words and phrases, but as the setting up of these devices is quite critical they should only be used on the mix and never while recording. In this way it's possible for you to take as many passes as you need to get it right.

vocal equalisation

Vocals often need some equalisation to ensure that they sit well with the backing track, while excessively sibilant vocals may require dynamic equalisation with the use of a de-esser. No two singers have exactly the same voice characteristics, so any EQ treatment you employ will be different depending on the qualities of the singer. However, modifying the vast majority of voices in certain general areas of the audio spectrum can be considered appropriate, though final EQ settings will have to be tuned by ear while the singer is being recorded.

Any top boost should be applied quite high in the frequency spectrum, up at 6-15kHz, but watch out for sibilance creeping in. If the voice starts to sound harsh then try moving the EQ centre frequency higher. However, don't settle for a dull vocal sound simply because using the right EQ brings up the sibilance; if you have to use a de-esser to save the day then do it.

Boosting in the 1-2kHz range lends a rather honky, cheap sound to the vocals and so is not recommended, unless you're using it as a special effect. Try to keep vocals as flat as possible and bear in mind that, unless you have really high-quality outboard equalisers, adding more than a very small amount of EQ boost can spoil the sound.

Presence can be added with just a little boost at 3-4kHz, but be careful or the sound may become harsh. Vocals are the most natural sound in the world, so our ears soon register the fact that they've been tampered with.

If you're mixing several backing vocals then rolling off a touch of bass might help the vocal to sit better in the mix without sounding muddy. On its own the equalised backing vocal might sound thin, but once in the mix the chances are that it will sound fine, and it won't fill up the vulnerable lower mid area of the spectrum with unwanted energy.

double-tracked vocals

Double tracking is a popular treatment for adding depth to a voice. It may be used to compensate for a weak voice or to add impact to choruses and so on. Traditionally, the singer performs the same part twice (or more) on separate tracks, and the tracks are then played back together to give the effect of two or more vocalists singing in unison. An effect simulated with delay or chorus rarely sounds as good as the real thing.

A common problem with double-tracked parts is that words may start together but end up sounding ragged because the endings of the words aren't in sync.

Nowhere is this more evident than with words ending with 'T' or 'S' sounds. One way around this is to perform the second take in a deliberately sloppy manner by missing off or fading the ends of tricky words. Then, when the two tracks are played together, the result will sound much tighter. The same applies to backing harmony vocal parts.

To create a little difference between the two vocal lines, the multitrack can be speeded up or down by around a semitone before the second part is recorded, which will give the voice a different character when the tape is returned to normal speed. This is a trick often used by writers of radio jingles to create the effect of a large vocal group when overdubbing just one or two singers.

Another useful technique is to use a delay line to delay the headphone mix by around 50ms when recording the second track. This has the effect of making the singer perform the second part 50ms later than the first part, which produces a short delay effect when the tape is replayed normally. This technique produces a rich vocal effect without compromising the quality of the sound – the material which is recorded doesn't actually pass through the delay unit, so any old delay box will do the trick.

fake double tracking

Inevitably, some singers can never perform a song the same way twice. In this case, any attempt at double tracking will sound messy and unacceptable. This is where ADT (Automatic Double Tracking) comes to the rescue, and because it's applied after the performance it's something that can be tried at the mixing stage.

This effect was originally set up by using an open-reel analogue recorder running at high speed to function as a delay unit with a very short delay, or by using the short delay setting on a tape echo unit. Fine tuning the delay so that the original sound and its repeat just start to separate from each other gives the effect of two voices singing slightly out of time with each other.

The effect isn't entirely convincing because the pitching of the delayed part is exactly the same as the original, but using later devices which simulate the effect with chorus or pitch-shifting circuitry can sound rather more realistic. Here are some ideas to try out.

- Add a short delay of between 30ms and 100ms to the sound but either subtly chorus the delay or process it via a pitch shifter to give a detuning effect of between five and ten cents (one cent is one hundredth of a semitone).

- Extra depth can be added by panning the original and delayed signals to opposite sides of the stereo mix.

- If you have a basic DDL that has a modulation section you can use this to delay the sound and vary the pitch simultaneously, in effect using it as a kind of delayed chorus setting. After judging an accurate delay time by ear, adjust the modulation depth and speed so that the pitch-wavering effect is just audible – a modulation rate of 2-3Hz combined with a very shallow modulation depth should do the trick nicely. The longer the delay time the less modulation depth you'll need to create the required degree of pitch shifting.

reverb and ambience

Picking the right reverb setting is really a matter of taste. Here are a few guidelines you could follow, however, which are based largely on common sense.

- Bright reverb settings give the vocal an attractive 'sizzle', as long as they are not bright enough to bring the level of sibilance up to an unacceptable degree.

- If the song you're recording is a ballad, a longer, softer reverb might create an appropriate atmosphere.

- Short ambience settings rich in early reflections can be used to add life to a vocal, while there is also a place for both adding little or no perceptible reverb at all and using trick settings, such as reverse reverb, as long as they are used in moderation.

advanced reverb effects

You can create a useful effect by configuring a DDL to give a single repeat of between 50ms and 100ms and then feeding this into a reverb unit to give a pre-delay. This creates a deeper sense of space and also separates the reverb from the basic sound a little, which can enhance the clarity of the sound. Many multi-effects units have a pre-delay setting included in the reverb parameters, but this little dodge is still useful on those occasions when your main reverb unit is tied up with another task and you have to create an effect with an effects box that offers only preset settings or a limited range of adjustments.

A wider reverb effect can be achieved by positioning a delay after the reverb yet on only one of the stereo outputs. This splits the reverb so that it starts in one speaker and then moves over to the other. This treatment again adds a sense of movement but is not too obvious or gimmicky. Figure 3.2 illustrates how it might be arranged.

reverb panning

Reverb panning can also be used to create movement and generate interest without actually sounding too gimmicky, and if your multi-effects unit is capable then panning the output of the reverb unit from left to right (ideally at a rate that fits in with the tempo of the song) can be very effective. If you don't have a panner then you can create the same effect by using a gate that has side-chain or key inputs. The pan effect is triggered via percussive sounds programmed into a drum machine (which must have the means to separate the two sounds,

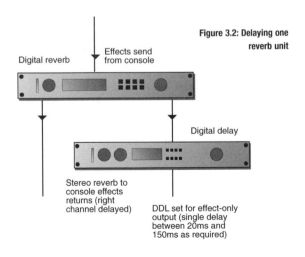

Figure 3.2: Delaying one reverb unit

Digital reverb

Effects send from console

Digital delay

Stereo reverb to console effects returns (right channel delayed)

DDL set for effect-only output (single delay between 20ms and 150ms as required)

even if only by panning them to opposite outputs). The two channels of the gate are triggered alternately by feeding in these drum hits via their key inputs, and ideally the drum machine would be synchronised to the master tape with a MIDI sequencer. The stereo reverb is then fed into the main gate inputs, and the attack and release times are set to give a smooth pan. This only takes a few attempts to set up and is remarkably effective. Figure 3.3 shows how a gate can be used as a reverb panner.

If you have two reverb units then try applying a reverse setting on one and a conventional reverb setting on the other. Pan one reverb unit left and the other right and you'll find that, as the normal reverb decays on one side, the reverse effect will build up on the other, giving a different kind of moving-pan effect.

a matter of taste

Almost any effect, no matter how bizarre, can be justified in context – it's all a matter of artistic judgment, which is where a good producer comes into his or her own. I've heard vocals chopped into short, gated sections and then panned between the speakers, giving the effect of a synchronised, intermittent fault in the mic cable, but because it was used sparingly and in the right place it worked. Drum sounds can be deliberately distorted via a guitar pre-amp or pedal, bass synth sounds can certainly be beefed up using distortion, and there are now so many weird sound-mangling software plug-ins that there's really no limit to the effects you can achieve. All you have to do is ask yourself whether the effect actually makes the song sound any better. Remember that the technology is there to serve you, not the other way around.

Also, try to avoid cliches unless you have a genuine artistic reason to use them. Adding repeat echo to the last

Figure 3.3: A gate used as a reverb panner

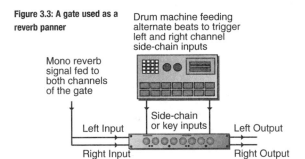

Drum machine feeding alternate beats to trigger left and right channel side-chain inputs

Mono reverb signal fed to both channels of the gate

Left Input

Side-chain or key inputs

Left Output

Right Input

Right Output

By setting a long attack and long release time the signal can be made to pan from one gate output to the other, although the exact settings will need to be adjusted to suit the tempo of the trigger inputs. Note that, on a gate with a dedicated ducking facility, panning may be achieved simply by setting one channel of the gate to duck and the other to normal gate operation. In this case the gate should be set for stereo operation, and only a single trigger input will be required word in a vocal line or the last word in a song is an often-abused trick, and it's generally more effective to attempt the unexpected than kill your music with predictability. If you must use a cliche then try to use it in an unexpected way or in an unusual place. For example, adding a gross repeat echo to the very first word in a song might have more impact than using it right at the end.

key vocal tips

Before leaving the subject, I've compiled a few tips that can be applied when recording and mixing vocals.

- Ensure that the singer is well rehearsed, physically comfortable and under no psychological pressure. Most perform best when standing in a room with a temperature that is comfortable but not too warm. If they are distracted by other members of the band or by hangers on, send everyone but the engineer (and producer, if you have one) out of the studio.

- Take the time to provide the vocalist with an accurate headphone mix and add a little reverb to help them sing more confidently. It will make life a lot easier if you can rig up a system whereby the vocalists can adjust their own monitor level. A good headphone mix will help to encourage a good performance.

- Always set up a pop shield between the singer and the microphone, as failure to do so will almost certainly result in pops on plosive 'B' and 'P' sounds which can't be fixed afterwards. The pop shield may be a commercial model or it may be a DIY job, comprising stocking material stretched over a wire coat-hanger frame or even a fine metal or plastic sieve or chip-pan splashguard. Any of these will do the job without affecting the tone of the mic. Foam wind shields, however, are virtually useless in combating pops.

- Use a good microphone. You don't need to use anything too exotic, but you should use nothing less than a good stage dynamic mic. Professional studios generally use capacitor microphones, but in the project studio a good back-electret mic or even a good dynamic vocal mic can produce excellent results.

- Choose a mic that will suit the singer. Singers with thin or excessively bright voices may actually sound better with a dynamic mic, while those with voices that need more of an open sound may benefit from a capacitor or back-electret mic. If you have several models from which to choose then perform a test recording with each and pick the one which has the most flattering effect on the singer's voice.

- Use the right mic pickup pattern. Most project studio vocal recordings are made using a cardioid or unidirectional mic, as these pick up less sound from the sides and the rear. However, good omni mics generally exhibit a more natural, open sound, which is useful when working with a singer with a nasal or boxy voice. If you work a couple of inches closer to an omni mic you'll approach the same direct-sound-to-room-sound ratio you'd get with a cardioid.

- Position the mic carefully. If the singer is too close to the mic then the risk of popping will increase and the level will change noticeably every time he or she moves slightly. Cardioid mics also exhibit a bass boost proximity effect which varies as the singer moves to and from the mic. On the other hand, if the singer is too far away from the mic then the room reflections will colour the sound, making it seem remote and boxy. As a rule, a mic distance of around six to twelve inches or 15-24cm is ideal.

- Minimise the room's influence on the sound. The mic picks up both direct sound from the singer and reflected sound from the room. Minimise room reflection by keeping away from the walls and using screens (which can be improvised from sleeping bags or blankets) behind and to the sides of the singer.

- Use mic technique to control the level. If the singer pulls back from the mic slightly when singing louder notes there will be less risk of overloading the recorder or mic pre-amp, and you won't need to use as much compression to even things up. An experienced singer may also lean into the mic on quiet, intimate passages to exploit the proximity effect. However, to prevent an inexperienced singer from moving too close to the mic you should position the pop shield about three inches from the mic.

- Stand mount the microphone if possible. Only allow the singer to hold the mic if their musical performance would otherwise be compromised. If a singer wants to hold the mic by hand, particularly if it's a cardioid model, keep the hand clear of the rear of the basket as an obstruction in this area can change both the mic's directional and tonal characteristics.

- Don't settle for anything less than the best vocal performance, and don't expect a perfect first take. You'll often have to punch in and out around phrases that need further takes, but if you have enough tracks then persuade the vocalist to sing the whole song several times and then compile a track from the best parts of each take. Hard-disk editing is much more flexible than tape editing in this respect.

- Use suitable compression. I've already stressed the importance of compression, but you should also be aware that some compressors can be used to have a creative effect on the sound rather than simply to keep the level under control. If the singer's voice needs to sound more 'up front' then a compressor with musically beneficial side-effects may be the best choice, such as one of the many tube and opto compressors currently available on the market.

- Don't overdo equalisation. EQ only sounds decent on most budget desks when used sparingly or when used to cut unwanted frequencies. Mid-range boosting usually results in the sound becoming nasal or phasey, so try to use as little EQ as you can. Try a different mic and position it differently before reaching for the EQ.

- Use reverb sparingly. Vocals recorded in a dry acoustic environment need reverb to give them a sense of space and reality, but don't use more than the song really needs. As a general rule, busy songs need less reverb while you can afford to use more on slow ballads with considerable space in their arrangement. Listen to some commercial records of a similar style to your own and try to determine the reverb techniques which the producer has used.

- Even if the vocals are recorded cleanly, using a bright reverb setting can introduce sibilance that isn't noticeable on a dry sound. Instead of de-essing the vocals (which often ends up sounding unnatural), try de-essing only the feed to the reverb unit.

- When using prominent echo or delay effects, try to get them in time with the song, either by calculating the delay needed to match the tempo or by using the tap-tempo facility if one is provided. For a less obviously rhythmic echo, try a multitap delay with irregular tap spacings.

- To ensure that the vocal is mixed at the right level in the song, listen to the mix from outside the room and check that the song has the same balance as something you might hear on the radio. The vocals are the most important part of the song and so must be positioned well forward, but not so far forward that they sound stuck onto the backing.

- Experiment with some of the techniques discussed here when you're not working against the clock. Take note of anything that works particularly well so that you can recreate the effect when you need it.

balancing

Now it's about time to put some of the tips and techniques learned from the previous chapters into practice. It would be a mistake to expect to get a perfect balance within minutes in the way that an experienced professional might, but if you take your time then you should obtain some good results.

Before starting to mix it helps to organise sounds into logical groups. This can be done by routing sounds within a specific group (such as all of the drums in a drum kit, or a group of backing vocals) to a specific pair of subgroups so that, once balanced, the whole kit can be controlled by using just a couple of faders, which means that you then don't need as many faders to handle the mix.

balance

The most important part of mixing is striking a balance between the various sounds, and if the basic tracks have been recorded properly it should initially be possible to set up a reasonable balance without resorting to EQ. Effects need not be added right away, but it helps to have the necessary effects units patched in and ready for use, and adding some vocal reverb will provide colour. You should switch the EQ to Bypass on those channels on which it isn't being used, and ensure that any unused mixer channels are not only muted but also unrouted – in other words, all of the routing buttons should be in their up position. This will prevent the channel from contributing to the mix buss noise of the console and will help in obtaining a quieter final mix. All unused aux sends should be set at zero level, and the loudest sends should be around three quarters up. Noise can be reduced if care is taken over setting levels.

If your console allows trim at mixdown then all inputs should be trimmed using the PFL metering system. Likewise, the input levels of all of the effects units should be checked. Having attended to these basics, my preferred way of working is to sort out the drum and bass balance first. This should not be refined too much, however, as the apparent balance will change once the rest of the instruments and voices are in the mix. When the rhythm section sounds good, the remaining faders can be brought up one at a time until a reasonable overall balance has been achieved. It's only when all instruments are in place that you should start to worry about the finer points of EQ and balance, as things can sound very different when they are heard in isolation.

Some engineers and producers insist that the only way to work is to put all of the faders up to start with and then adjust for a balance. It depends on what works best for the individual, however, so if you're lucky enough to be able to work this way then that's fine. However, I've spoken to many well-regarded engineers and producers who admit that they don't have this natural gift for balance and therefore have to work just as hard as the rest of us!

using stereo

Once you've achieved a reasonable balance you can then begin working on the effects and the stereo positioning of the different sounds. Bass drums, bass guitars and bass synths are invariably panned to the centre to anchor the mix and to spread the load of these high-energy frequencies over both speakers. Similarly, lead vocals are usually positioned at centre stage, because that's where we expect the vocalist to be.

The position of backing vocals is less rigid, however; they can be split so that some are left and some are

right, they can be left in the centre, or they can all be
grouped in one off-centre position. I like to hear
different backing vocal lines coming in from different
sides, but this decision is purely personal and there is
no absolute right and wrong. If recorded vocals
exhibit any sibilance, a de-esser should be patched in
before proceeding.

When the mix is almost there it can be very helpful to
listen to the balance from an adjacent room with the
adjoining door left open. Although I can find no logical
explanation for the phenomenon, any slight balance
problems show up starkly when a mix is auditioned in
this way, and most engineers and producers who have
discovered this method of checking a mix use it regularly.

level correction

A good mix will almost work without you having to
move the faders after setting the initial balance, but it's
more likely that some parts will need minor level
corrections throughout the mix. Obvious examples are
instrumental solos and changes in effects levels, but
even on vocals with heavy compression it may still be
necessary to adjust the occasional vocal phrase by a
decibel or two so that it sits properly. If the mix is
conducted manually then responsibility for adjusting

the faders can be shared amongst the band members. The level settings should be clearly marked with wax pencil, and each person should be aware of the time positions at which levels have to be changed. These changes can be handled automatically if an automated mixing system is available.

If the end of a track requires a fadeout, this may be performed manually or with an autofader. Fades are seldom shorter than 15 seconds and they may be as long as 30, so it's important to ensure that there is enough recorded material to cover the duration of the fade. If you know in advance that an album is to be compiled using a hard-disk editing system then it might be wiser to leave the fades until the final editing stage, when they can be controlled more precisely and can be faded into true silence.

I've already emphasised that setting the levels correctly on your console will help minimise noise, but we also have to deal with noise that is part of the recorded sound, including breath noise from singers, hum and hiss from guitar amps and digital background noise from synths, samplers and drum machines. If sequenced MIDI instruments are being used it's often possible to program changes in level via MIDI, but care must be taken because some instruments emit a more or less constant level of noise, regardless of the level of the voice currently playing. It's always important to use these machines as close to their maximum volume setting as is practical, as this will usually give the best signal-to-noise ratio. Likewise, it's possible to mute instruments via the sequencer, but this just stops the sequenced parts from playing and doesn't affect the background noise in any way.

gates and mutes

Gates or expanders are very effective in cleaning up noise in electronic instruments, though care must be taken to match the release time of the gate to the sound being processed so that the natural decay of the sound isn't cut short. In some cases it may be possible to use a pair of gates over a stereo subgroup, as fewer gates will then be needed to process the mix. It must be remembered, however, that gates can only keep the noise down during pauses and can do nothing when a signal is present.

Perhaps the most dramatic effect of MIDI muting or gating can be noticed right at the beginning of the song, where there is silence until the first note is played. It shouldn't be necessary to mute every short silence, but it's a good idea to mute the vocal track during instrumental solos or bridge sections and to mute the lead guitar track both before and after the solo. As a rule, muting as many tracks that aren't playing as possible will result in a cleaner-sounding mix.

Muting on the MIDI console can be very useful for dealing with source noise, and although it may take a little time to set up the results are usually well worth the trouble. It is necessary to go through each tape track and set up the mute points individually, but once they're right they'll still be right every time you run the mix. If you can arrange muting and unmuting on a beat it may help to disguise any discontinuity or change in noise level.

The mutes on most MIDI desks are very quiet, but on some older analogue models there is an audible click if several mute buttons are pressed at the same time. If this is the case, it should be possible to work around the problem by using the mutes on the subgroups or master output faders rather than attempting to switch all of the channels at once.

noise filters

If some of your sound sources are noticeably noisy, even when being played, it might be useful to employ a single-ended noise-reduction unit. These are generally analogue dynamic filter units that filter out higher frequencies as sounds decay. If used carefully they can bring about a dramatic decrease in noise without affecting the sound of the wanted signal, although they tend to affect the tail ends of long reverbs or gradual decays, so it's probably prudent to assign all of the noisy sounds to a stereo subgroup and process only this group. This means that the higher-quality sounds and effects returns will remain unprocessed, providing a more natural-sounding result. You should experiment with the threshold settings as the music plays to make sure that there are no noticeable tonal changes. A correctly-set single-ended noise-reduction unit only affects the signal when the levels are very low – if you can hear the background hiss changing in level as the music plays then you know you're applying too much processing.

getting a produced sound

It's all very well learning about balance and effects, but how do the professionals get their records sounding so polished and 'produced'? Some people assume that the superior equipment used in pro studios is the answer, but, although it's true that you need competent gear to do the job properly, you don't actually need anything esoteric. Even when it comes to recording vocals you don't have to use a high-end tube capacitor mic – a number of top artists use relatively inexpensive dynamic models, simply because that's what works best for them. A few years ago demos were given away by the drum sound, but now there are good drum machines, drum samples and sample loops as well as real drums available, and mixing acoustic and sampled drums also works well.

The secret of arriving at a produced sound starts with the musical arrangement – it doesn't matter what you do to your recording afterwards if the source material isn't up to scratch. Accurate timing and tuning should be a given, but the choice of sounds and the way in which acoustic instruments and voices are recorded also has a huge bearing on the quality of the end result. For example, if vocals are recorded in a small, untreated room, the chances are that the resulting sound will be boxy, so if you position your mic somewhere near (but not exactly in) the centre of a larger room and erect improvised screens (fashioned from sleeping bags, duvets, blankets and so on), this will help to kill the reflections. If these precautions are adopted, virtually any respectable microphone will provide you with good results, as long as you use a pop shield. It's also possible to record acoustic guitars in the same environment.

We've already seen that vocals invariably need compression, but what kind and how much? Listen to what you've recorded and try to establish the amount of variation in the vocal level. If there is lot of level variation then it might be better to use a compressor that can fix the level without changing the sound too much. The compressors that come as standard in certain digital mixers are good for this, along with those in some analogue models, as the gain reduction can really be piled on without the sound changing too radically. On the other hand, you may feel that the vocal line needs thickening as well as levelling, in which case you might find that a compressor with character might be better suited to performing the task. Tube and opto compressors generally produce the fattest sounds, and of course there are software plug-ins that emulate just about anything you can buy in a rack box.

The aim is to get the vocal line sitting nicely with the backing track so that you don't get the urge to turn it up or down in different parts of the song. Professional engineers may spend some time fine tuning vocal levels with their mix automation systems even after they've set up the compressors, and you can do the same if you use either a digital mixer or a computer-based recording system.

Poorly-recorded guitars and basses can be a giveaway. Sticking a mic in front of an amp is still probably the best way to get a live-sounding rendition of the performance, but there are now so many good recording pre-amps around that there's little excuse for recording a thin or buzzy guitar sound. Go easy on the overdrive, however, and consider using less of it, combined with compression, if you need sustain. Use a gate to keep your guitar tracks clear of noise and stay well away from computer monitors when recording, as these often interfere with guitar signals and cause hum.

If two guitars are playing essentially the same chords, you should first decide if two guitars are actually necessary. If you feel that they are, consider using different chord inversions for one of the parts or even use a capo. (Acoustic guitars almost always sound better miked than DI'd.)

Basses can actually be more difficult to record than guitars because, although they may sound great in isolation, when DI'd via an active DI box and a compressor they may still lack punch in the context of the mix. Again, consider miking the amp or using a guitar DI pre-amp so that just a little overdrive can be added to warm up the sound. Compression will help to keep the sound even and punchy, and a tip here is to make any necessary EQ adjustments when the rest of the track is playing, as in this way you'll be able to make the sound match the track. If you EQ the sound first, it might sound great on its own but it may then become completely lost when the other faders are up.

synth sounds

Synth sounds have to be chosen with care, as a lot of factory patches are designed to sound large and impressive for the benefit of those who choose their new instruments on the strength of preset cruising. What sounds wonderful on its own might take up too much space in a mix. If you don't like the idea of editing the patch, however, try using EQ to trim off excess bass or high end. The EQ'd patch might sound odd in isolation but it may sound more appropriate in the mix. Another tip for those reluctant to get into heavy editing is to layer patches in order to obtain the desired result. For example, a deep bass sound mixed with a more percussive patch might help to produce a bass that can be heard as well as felt.

It's important not to over-orchestrate arrangements, especially when fat synth pads and overdriven guitars are used at the same time. The same is true of some treated drum loops, which can actually take up a lot of space. If in doubt, listen to a few commercial songs which have been mixed in a similar style – you may be surprised at how little is going on at any one time. Again, it will help if you can record your sounds as accurately as possible at source so that you don't need to add much EQ. There are few budget mixers that are equipped with the kind of EQ that works well in exercising major tonal changes, and often you'll find that your mix becomes harsher, boomier or less focused if you use more EQ.

effects and space

Once you've created your space, don't waste it all by filling every available gap with heavy reverb. Applying heavy reverb to a sound will push it to the back of a mix, so if you want a vocal to appear in the front of a mix you should use a fairly bright reverb with around 80ms of pre-delay. You should also avoid overdoing the decay time, especially with faster songs. Other effects should also be used carefully – use an effect because the track needs it, not because you happen to have it! Some effects can sound even more dramatic if they are used for short sections of a song instead of being used full-on all the way through, and delay effects often work best when the delay time is related to the tempo of the song.

handling bass

Bass sounds are very important in modern music, but it's important to appreciate that not every listener has large studio monitors at home. This means that, when mixing, you have to decide whether your mix needs to sound large when played over a full-range club PA system or whether it should sound best on domestic speakers. If you want it to sound good when played back on both, you'll need to compromise. For example, cathedral organs produce bass notes right down to 20Hz or even lower, which can resonate through your entire body when reproduced through a full-range, high-power system, but if you try to replay these sounds through a typical music system you're unlikely to hear very much at all, as most of the energy falls below the lowest frequency that the speaker can generate. However, very low frequencies still use up system headroom, which means that they can actually be counterproductive – they will reduce the maximum level at which you can play back the sounds which you can hear.

In practical terms, this means that, if you want powerful bass that works in a domestic listening environment, it's pretty pointless going much below 40Hz, as most hi-fi systems don't even reproduce sound this low. In fact most smaller systems start to roll off at 80Hz or even higher, so you need to make sure that there's plenty of energy in the 70-90Hz range in order for the bass to work on pretty much all domestic systems. With this in mind, you can create or adapt existing synth bass sounds so that they will sound better over small speakers.

synth bass

Synth waveforms that are close to sine or triangle waves produce a very strong fundamental with few harmonics, so to make sounds audible on small speakers as well you could try using a waveform that has plenty of harmonics, such as a square wave or ramp wave, and then use your synth's low-pass filter to trim away any of the upper harmonics that you don't want. Harmonically-rich sounds always appear to be louder than pure tones, but if they're too rich they'll eat up all of the space in your mix.

Alternatively, start out with a near sinusoidal or triangular waveform and then add harmonics by distorting it with a guitar recording pre-amp, preferably one with a speaker simulator to round out the less musical high-frequency distortion. One advantage of using a distortion device is that the added harmonics follow the dynamics of the signal so that you get most distortion where the bass sound is loudest. Also, because distortion usually involves an element of clipping or limiting, it may also help in controlling excessive peak levels.

Another approach to creating sound is to use two oscillators, one pitched an octave below the other. This ensures that there is plenty of energy at both the fundamental and an octave above it. The amount of the higher oscillator should then be adjusted until the sound has the right combination of depth and definition. It's also effective to layer a more percussive sound with the deep bass patch, such as another synth sound (including filtered noise) or a true percussion sound such as a bass drum, deep tom or hi-hat. It may also help to lengthen the attack of the percussive sound slightly to make it less drumlike. Deep sounds can usually be made considerably longer than higher, more percussive elements.

There are some computer-based bass enhancement programs that attenuate low fundamentals while adding psychoacoustically-calculated harmonics, which are designed to increase the listener's ability to perceive bass over small speakers. These sound more impressive over smaller speakers than over full-range systems and so are probably best reserved for mixes designed to be replayed on a home stereo system, though you can keep some of the low fundamentals (at a lower level) if you want to make a compromise mix. This technique is based on the proven psychoacoustic principle that the human hearing system has the ability to mentally recreate missing or attenuated fundamental frequencies from the remaining harmonics.

To add a truly deep bass, use a processor such as the dbx boom box, which adds real subharmonics an octave below an existing bass sound. Such machines should be used carefully, however, as some of the bass frequencies generated could damage small or under-powered speakers, including studio monitors. This technique is probably used best in mixing rather than in replaying music in clubs or at home.

Regardless of how you create your bass sounds, they should be panned to the centre of your mix so that the load of reproducing these difficult low frequencies is shared equally between the two stereo speakers.

maximum bass

Use a dynamic equaliser, if you have one, to produce extra bass boost when bass notes are playing. Because this may increase the actual level of the bass sound significantly, a limiter or compressor, set to a high ratio, should be used after the filter to avoid losing control over the level of the bass signal. The dynamic equaliser can prove to be particularly effective when treating a track that's already been mixed, as it can beef up the bass without affecting the other sounds in the mix too much.

It's also possible to compress synthetic sounds, but in either case it's wise to use a separate limiter (or a compressor with an independent limiter section) to control the peak level. The perceived volume will be greater because the compressor increases the average signal level.

Even though the sound may appear to be fine in isolation you could still try adding mild distortion because, as well as making deep sounds seem more punchy, distortion also makes instruments sound louder. Often a limp bass guitar line can be revived by adding a little amp-style overdrive. If you don't have a guitar pre-amp or a tube processor that can be overdriven then see if there's a software equivalent amongst the plug-ins that came with your MIDI/audio sequencer.

bass and mastering

Much can be achieved at the mastering stage, and a professional mastering engineer will be able to reduce the level of excessive deep bass without affecting the way in which the mix will sound over a typical hi-fi unit. Compression, dynamic EQ and more selective parametric equalisation may also be brought to bear during mastering, and, as recent reviews have shown, this type of work can be undertaken at home with a reasonable degree of success by using one of the newer all-in-one mastering processors or suitable mastering software. There's a lot more to obtaining a big bass sound than simply choosing a low-pitched bass sound and then turning it up loud, especially when you're mixing a track to be replayed over a domestic hi-fi system. The choice of the source sound, its volume envelope, compression and equalisation/filtering all play a part, and it also helps to have some idea of the psychoacoustics of bass perception. The human ear can be fooled into perceiving a fundamental that is completely absent if the higher harmonics are present in the correct proportions (which is why you can still convey the impression of bass from a small transistor radio), but if you want to record bass that can be felt over a large club system then the fundamental needs to be present as well as the harmonics. If you're mixing with clubs in mind, it's therefore important that you have either a full-range monitoring system or access to a club sound system on which to check your mixes. If you rely on near-field monitors you'll know what to expect on a domestic hi-fi, but you'll have no idea of what the bass end will do over a club system. Obtaining the best results will involve a degree of experimentation, especially if you're after a compromise mix that will sound decent in both clubs and homes, but experimentation is important as it drives progress and makes it more likely that you will come up with a distinctive sound of your own. If it is the case that you need a compromise mix then your best approach is to keep some true deep bass but to go easy on the levels. The higher harmonics also need to be present to make sure that the bass is audible on a domestic system, so use a mix of both approaches and balance them until you find a compromise that sounds acceptable in all listening environments.

mastering

Many people don't realise the effect of mastering on commercial records. Before they are mastered, however, you might be surprised just how ordinary some mixes sound. In the commercial world mixing and mastering are two very separate processes, whereas in the project studio you may need to handle both yourself. Mastering often involves nothing more than compression, limiting and equalisation, but it sounds more effective because of the quality of the equipment being used and the expertise of the person using it. This is one area in which the quality of the equipment makes a huge difference, even though now, with all-in-one mastering processors now available at prices project studio owners can afford, it's possible to obtain a professional sound at home, as long as you have accurate ears and monitors.

A good equaliser doesn't just change the spectral balance of a sound; it also seems to lift information out of a mix. A popular technique in mastering is the application of an overall boost of just one or two decibels at around 15kHz with a wide bandwidth setting, which is what people mean when they talk about air EQ, sheen or gloss. With a high-quality equaliser this will lift out high-end detail while at the same time pulling the vocals forward, but it shouldn't make the sound harsh or toppy. Similarly, applying a gentle dip at around 180-250Hz may help clarify a muddy lower mid range, while boost applied at 70-90Hz will firm up a weak bass end. It is vital to use a classy equaliser for this job, though – a cheap model just won't deliver the necessary magic!

A very gentle overall compression of around 1.1:1, with a threshold of -30dB to -40dB, will make a mix sound more even and powerful. However, multiband mastering processors add a lot of flexibility in the area of compression because they allow you to do things like apply more compression to the bass end than to the rest of the mix. This helps firm up the bass end without affecting the sound of the rest of the mix, and any spectral imbalance caused by the different compression ratios can be restored by adjusting the levels of the various frequency bands at the compressor output.

Mastering also tends to involve limiting, which is a process similar to compression (albeit with an infinitely high ratio) that controls just the tips of loud peaks. By applying a little limiting it's often possible to increase the average level of a mix by several decibels without any side-effects becoming audible. Starting from a 20- or 24-bit master and then reducing to a 16-bit master right at the end of the process uses more bits on the final CD, which means less noise, less distortion and better low-level resolution. It also makes your CD sound as loud as the 'produced' commercial CDs in your collection. It's important to use a limiter specifically designed for mastering, be it software or hardware in nature, and to avoid over-limiting, or you will compromise the overall sound of the mix. Usually four or five decibels of limiting is all that's needed.

Processing your mix via tube circuitry can also warm it up, which is why tube EQs and compressors are popular for use in mastering. The secret with all of these treatments is to use them sparingly and to always compare the processed with the unprocessed sound to make sure that you haven't used them to excess. A good processor will transform a recording with just a couple of decibels of adjustment where needed. If you find that you're using a lot of processing then your basic mix may be too wide of the mark.

Successful musical production isn't something that's just painted on at some point in the recording process; it's the result of a continual attention to detail at all points throughout the recording and mixing processes, beginning with the musical arrangement and choice of sounds. Nevertheless, processing at the mastering stage (ie after the mix) can make a huge difference. Professional mastering is expensive, however, and for two very good reasons: the professionals have great equipment and a lot of experience in using it. If you're not confident that you have the necessary equipment and expertise to do your mix justice then consider getting your work professionally mastered, especially if it's destined for commercial release. However, if you're going to do this, don't process your final mix at all – leave each track just as it is.

On the other hand, if your mix is 95% complete and you just don't have the budget available for professional mastering, don't be dissuaded from having a go at mastering your material yourself. There are now several hardware and software mastering processors on the market that are within the financial reach of many project studio owners. Remember, however, that it's a question of listening carefully to decide what's actually needed rather than working to a formula.

monitoring alternatives

Before a final mix is approved it should be checked on different speaker systems, including car systems and domestic hi-fis. Large studio monitoring systems can be very misleading, and it's essential to test the mix at a moderate listening level on a pair of small speakers. You shouldn't bow to the temptation of mixing at too high a volume as this will only serve to adversely affect your ability to judge the sound. Ultimately, the best way of checking is to listen to your mix at the same level at which you would expect the listener to hear it.

the master tape

DAT has become a standard mastering medium, and if possible you should master at a sampling frequency of 44.1kHz, as the sample rate then won't then need to be converted a CD master is made. Keep a very close eye on recording levels because there is no leeway above 0VU – the sound immediately clips and distortion is usually audible. Try to arrange your levels so that the peaks reach between -3VU and -6VU on the DAT machine's meters, which should provide an adequate safety margin while still providing a good signal-to-noise performance.

The master tape must be backed up once it has been recorded, particularly if it is on DAT (contrary to some expectations, DAT isn't 100% reliable). To back up one DAT on another, make a clone by connecting the machines via their digital audio links. It's important to use a proper digital cable to do this rather than an audio lead. It's safest to leave at least ten seconds of unrecorded tape at the beginning of a DAT (if trouble is going to occur, it usually occurs here), and the backup should be clearly marked and stored in a safe place.

It's also worth backing up DAT masters to other media, such as open-reel analogue tape, CD-R or DVD RAM/ROM. Interestingly, in many cases an analogue copy sounds better than the DAT, even though the noise performance won't be as good! This is undoubtedly due to the many small imperfections of analogue recording that contribute to its warm, comfortable sound.

labelling

All session tapes should be clearly labelled, as should any unused mixes and out-takes that you may wish to keep. You should include on the label such information as:

- The track format.
- The tape speed.
- The noise-reduction system used.

- Track titles.
- Track start times and end times.
- Track durations.

Although calibration tones shouldn't be necessary with DAT, tape duplicators and mastering houses like to have a 1kHz tone recorded at the start of a tape, at around 20 seconds in duration and at a level of -10VU. The actual level is less important than making a note of it on the box!

If the master tape is intended for album production then the individual tracks must spaced apart by the required duration of silence. With analogue tape this is achieved by splicing lengths of plastic leader tape or blank recording tape between the songs, with the length of the splice depending on how the previous song ends and how the next one starts. For example, the space required after a song with a fadeout ending might need to be only a couple of seconds, but if one songs ends with a bang and the next starts equally abruptly then anything up to five seconds might be needed. There are no hard-and-fast rules concerning this, but you can usually instinctively feel if a gap is more than half a second too short or long.

Spacing songs is less straightforward on a DAT tape than on an analogue tape because you can't stop and start DATs in the same instant way as analogue machines. By using two DAT machines it's possible to make a reasonable attempt at compiling an album simply by using the pause button on the second machine to start and stop it, but it's difficult to time gaps to an accuracy of better than one second. It's better to use a hard-disk editing system, which can time the gaps to accuracy of a millisecond and eliminate the noise before and after songs with surgical precision. These systems can usually handle fade-outs and -ins, level changes, and often digital equalisation, compression and limiting, very precisely.

difficult mix checklist

If you're having difficulty in obtaining a mix that sounds right, address the following points.

• Try to get an initial rough mix without using EQ or effects and then work from there. Also check that the mix sounds good in mono.

• Is there too much going on at once? Do you need all of those parts? If you do, can you afford to have some of them lower in the mix?

• Are mid-range sounds cluttering up the mix or overlapping with the bass sounds? If so, try using low-frequency shelving EQ to thin them out. They might sound odd in isolation but are more likely to sound right with the rest of the mix. Try shaving some bottom end from a pad synth part or acoustic guitar rhythm line to clean up the low-mid region.

- If you're still having difficulty, balance the drum and bass sounds first and then add the vocals and main instruments. You'll probably find that the mix sounds 90% there with just drums, bass, chords and vocals.

- If you're working with a sequencer, try using alternative pad or keyboard sounds if those you've chosen appear to be taking up too much space.

- Use effects sparingly. Add reverb where it sounds good, not simply where you feel it ought to be. Often the restrained use of effects produces the best results.

- Pan instruments and effects to their positions after you've made sure that the balance works in mono.

- Remember that some improvement can be expected at the mastering stage, especially if you are employing the services of a professional, but don't assume that this gives you an excuse to execute a sloppy mix, so do the best you possibly can. The mastering engineer will then be able to deliver that extra bit of magic.

mix automation

While most cheap analogue mixers must be operated manually, today's digital mixers and software recording and mixing systems are invariably capable of a degree of mix automation. However, a number of analogue studio consoles are also fitted with automation, using either motorised faders or computer-controlled VCAs (Voltage-Controlled Amplifiers).

The advantages of mix automation are fairly obvious. With manual mixing you only need to make one wrong move on a fader and you'll either have to start the mix again from the top or edit together the best sections from several mixes. With automated mixing, however, you can program all of the fader moves and correct any errors before allowing the computer to control the final mix.

analogue automation

The two most common methods of automating fader levels on analogue consoles are to use either motorised faders or voltage-controlled amplifiers controlled by standard manual faders. Either way, the automation is handled by a computer that may be either part of the mixer or an external unit. On a VCA system no audio signal passes through the faders – they're used only to produce a DC voltage, which is then read by the automation computer to determine the position of the faders. In contrast, a moving-fader system (which is only available on analogue consoles) routes the audio signal through the fader in the conventional manner.

The VCA approach was initially cheaper, as motorised faders were expensive, although this is no longer the case. The disadvantage of VCA systems, however, is that, because the faders don't move while the mix is being played back, there is no visual feedback of the actual levels unless you're using a system to which a computer monitor screen can be connected. A typical VCA system connected to a screen will often show both the physical position of the faders and the virtual fader levels corresponding to the VCA gain. If the mix data needs to be edited then the screen may be used to match up the actual fader levels to their virtual values in order to prevent sudden jumps in level at edit points, and on systems with no screen LEDs are often used – for example, a couple of up/down arrow-shaped lights next to the fader – to show the user the direction in which to move the fader in order to match the physical fader position to the stored VCA level.

Early VCA systems also compromised the sound and headroom of the console to some extent. Modern versions can be almost as good as a moving-fader system, however, with the added benefit that they don't go scratchy with age and dust.

moving faders

The moving-fader approach is arguably better in terms of visual feedback, because in an analogue console the fader level always relates to the actual gain setting of the channel. However, these systems can become noisy in exactly the same way as manual faders, and the mechanical noise of the faders moving during a mix can be distracting.

Virtually all analogue mixers that offer fader automation also have a system for automating channel mutes and sometimes effect send/return mutes as well. Mutes are a useful way of controlling noise, as the background hiss from 16 or more tracks soon adds up, regardless of how well they are recorded. In general, tracks should be muted when nothing is playing on them so that they don't contribute to the overall level of background noise. Mutes may also be used for artistic reasons, for example to remove recorded parts that are no longer required in a particular section of a song.

mix data

When a mix is being set up, the data generated by manual fader movements is stored in a computer. With more professional automation systems the computer will be dedicated to the mixer, but at the lower end of the market it's not unusual for the mix data to be sent in MIDI form so that it can be recorded into a regular MIDI sequencer. The level of sophistication of the equipment is an important factor in how easy it is to edit the mix data.

Once a rough mix has been written, the mix data on individual mixer channels may be replaced or modified in much the same way as performing a punch in on a multitrack tape recorder. In this way, a mix is fine tuned until everything is exactly right, and only then is the mix run to the master stereo recorder.

fader groups

On a manual analogue mixer it's necessary to use the desk's group buss faders to control the overall level of a subgroup while mixing. On an automated desk, however, whether VCA or moving fader, automated fader grouping can generally be handled without the need to involve the group buss fader or even to route all of the channels in the group to the same group buss. Once a number of faders have been assigned to a group, the levels of the entire group are adjusted by operating one of the faders in that group, maintaining any relative differences in level that have been set up. All of the faders in a group on a moving-fader desk will move when the controlling fader is moved, and if the scaling has been done properly then all of the faders will reach the bottom of their travel at the same time, regardless of their relative positions at the start of the fade.

VCA fader modes

When you first write a set of mix moves using a VCA console (it's conventional to discuss writing automation data rather than recording it), it's normal to use what's known as Absolute mode, in which the VCA levels correspond precisely to the positions of the faders. In contrast, the faders on a basic moving-fader analogue console always reflect the true channel gain setting, and so in effect they are always in Absolute mode. Figure 5.1 illustrates how the channel gain responds in Absolute mode.

Figure 5.1: How channel gain responds in Absolute mode

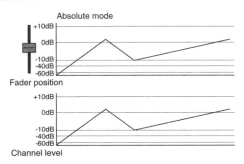

Figure 5.2: How levels behave in Offset mode

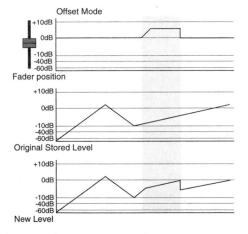

You may want to make further adjustments after the first rough mix has been written, but you may then find that, while some faders are at sensible positions somewhere near the middle of their travel, others are almost at the bottom. This is where another mode comes in, called Offset, Trim, or something similar, which allows the faders on a VCA console to be moved to more convenient midway positions (the 0dB position is most logical) without the VCA gains changing in turn. Then, when the mix is resumed, moving the faders in either direction from their new positions will increase or decrease the existing VCA values. When in this mode, written mix data doesn't replace the existing data but instead adds to it. This is very useful with a mix that's more or less perfect but has one or two phrases that need to be made louder or softer. All that you need to do here is switch to Offset mode, start writing mix data on the selected channel and then use the fader to lift or drop the level of the mix data that's already there. For example, if the fader is pushed up by 3dB, all of the existing mix data will be increased by 3dB. Figure 5.2 shows how levels behave in Offset mode.

Read mode

The console should be placed into Read mode when you want to play back your mix data. When a fader is in Write mode the gain is controlled by your fingers. When it's in

Read mode the computer calls the shots. Note, however, that, although Offset/Trim mode isn't available on moving-fader analogue consoles, it can be implemented on moving-fader digital consoles as no audio actually passes through the faders themselves.

Some consoles also have a mode that flips the channel from Read to Write mode if the fader is gripped during a mix playback. When the fader is released the channel reverts to Read mode. On a less expensive console it's more common to have a button associated with each channel that is the equivalent of the Record Select button on a multitrack recorder. Depending on the mixer, this button is used to arm individual channels (in which case you will have to select whether you want to write fader, mute or other data elsewhere in the system) or to punch in and out of Write mode for that channel. No two automation packages are exactly the same, although most follow similar basic rules, so it's essential that you read the manual for your automated desk before using it for a serious project.

snapshots

A snapshot (sometimes called a scene) is simply a set of automation data reflecting the state of the console gains and mutes at the time at which the snapshot was stored. On a digital console the snapshot may also include the pan, EQ, aux, effects and dynamics settings. If you're working on a complex mix that requires a lot of changes to take place instantaneously, it's often easier to create a snapshot and then call it up at the appropriate time (under the control of the automation) than to spend a lot of time editing the mix, changing lots of fader and mute settings. Most automated desks will be able to store a number of snapshots in their internal memory, which may be called up at any time during a mix as part of the normal automation process.

digital console automation

Digital consoles may be designed to emulate VCA-style automation (non-moving faders) or they may have moving faders, but because no audio passes through the faders on a digital desk you don't have the restriction that the faders must always correspond to the actual channel gain setting. Not only does this mean that a moving-fader desk can emulate VCA Offset modes but it also means that the faders can be switched off when necessary so that their noise and movement of their operation doesn't distract you. Unfortunately, not all moving-fader digital desks offer this latter facility.

While it's unusual to find an analogue console that offers automation of more than the channel levels, the mutes and the master stereo output level, modern digital consoles are designed to automate pretty much everything, including levels, pans, aux send/return levels, EQ, mutes – the whole works. What's more, most digital desks include one or more built-in digital effects, and often dynamic controls such as compression or gating, which are sometimes included on every channel. It's also possible, more often than not, to automate aspects of the effects and dynamics processors. Digital desks are also capable of grouping faders, and have the facility to store snapshots, frequently with features not found on analogue desks, such as the ability to morph from one snapshot to another over a period of time determined by the user.

You should be aware that Yamaha zero-series digital desks take a slightly different approach to most others, in that you can't just put the desk into Write mode and then start mixing. Instead you must create a snapshot or scene that represents the conditions at the very start of your mix and then write automation data from that point on. Further snaphots may then be introduced during the mix if required. In essence, your mix data comprises both automation and snapshot data.

synchronisation

Clearly, the console automation system has to keep time with your multitrack recorder or sequencer, and the conventional way of doing this is to run MTC or SMPTE, depending on the automation system you're using. On a system based around a multitrack recorder, the automation system is invariably used in Slave mode. (Actually, most mixer automation systems drop out of Write mode automatically when the timecode stops.)

saving mixes

Once a write pass has been made, you should then have the option either to update the stored mix with the new moves that have just been written or to abort the last pass and leave the mix as it was. You may also have the facility to store multiple mix histories, allowing you to return to any point in a project, or you may have only one mix which is constantly updated. In this latter case, it can be helpful to save some interim versions to disk. On some consoles it's possible to back up material via MIDI, so that mixes may be dumped to any suitable MIDI storage device or sequencer.

Software-based mixing environments often emulate their hardware counterparts, including the basic

Absolute and Offset modes, though other modes may also be included. Mix data is usually saved when the song is saved, so it's a good idea to save your material regularly. If you need to go back to older versions of the mix, save alternate versions of the song rather than always saving over the original.

using automation

It's sometimes difficult to know where to start when using mix automation, especially with digital consoles that allow you to automate almost everything. Those working with virtual studios inside their computers face a similar dilemma, as with these devices it's also possible to automate a huge number of mix parameters for both audio and MIDI tracks. The basic process of setting up a mix is basically the same on whatever system you choose to use. The main difference is that, on a computer, you can't drag more than one virtual fader at a time unless you have a hardware control interface.

It's probably true to say that the most important part of an automated mix happens before the automation is even switched on. With the mixer in Manual mode you should try to find a balance that sounds as close to what you're looking for as possible, then set your pan positions, make any EQ changes that are necessary and bring in your main effects, such as reverb. You should refer to the chapter on 'Mixing Tools' for guidelines on how to do this. You should also set up any effects that will be brought in during the course of the mix, such as tempo-related delays. If you have a console with on-board dynamics you can also set up any compression necessary for the main parts, and if you need to create fader groups then this is the time to do it.

So far you will have done no more than you would have done if you were mixing manually, but by spending time at this stage you'll be saving yourself a lot of time later. By now you should have a static mix in which the overall balance sounds good, but in which perhaps some notes or phrases are a little too loud or too quiet. There may also be parts playing throughout the mix that you'll want to take out, such as that heavy guitar part in the first verse. You may also have several takes of the main vocal and the instrumental solo on different tracks with a view to compiling a best take using sections of each, and if you're using a Yamaha digital mixer then you should save this basic mix as a scene or snapshot, as you will need to use the settings you've chosen as the starting point for your automation.

engaging automation

Probably the best place to start, once you've switched on your automation, is with the mutes. You should make sure that each track is muted when nothing is playing. You can also use mutes to compile parts from sections of takes recorded across several tracks by muting all parts except the one you want to hear. If you take your time in getting this right you'll be rewarded with a cleaner mix.

Once all of the mutes have been written, try closing your eyes and listening to the mix with the automation running things. In this way you'll be able to concentrate completely on the musical performance and check to make sure that you haven't missed anything. If you do come across anything, make notes of those places where the levels might need fine tuning. You'll often find the occasional vocal phrase sinking back into the mix or standing out too much, even if you've used compression to even out the mix as much as possible, but don't worry as fixing problems like these is where automation comes into its own. You may also find that you'd like to make small level changes for artistic reasons – for example, dropping an instrumental part by a decibel or so during the vocal part or slightly pumping up a support part during a solo.

All of these mental notes are translated into reality when the fader moves are written, and in most cases it's best to work on one fader at a time until the balance is correct all the way through the song. The first pass of fader moves is done in Absolute mode, but if you need to go back and refine your moves any further then you should use Offset mode, as it doesn't overwrite your existing mix data – it simply allows you to add to or subtract from the written material.

It's important that you save your mix at regular intervals, just in case your system crashes or you experience some other disaster, and always save your data before attempting anything in the least bit experimental. If you're editing a section of automation, try to ensure that the level is set at its original point or you might hear a sudden change in level at the punch-out point. As with audio recording, it's always safest to punch out of Automation mode during a pause rather than in the middle of a sound.

fine tuning

It's a good idea to listen to your mix with the automation running the mutes and faders in order to determine what else may be needed. For example, you may wish to bring up an echo send level at certain points in the song to add repeat echo, or you may choose to change some aspect of the EQ for part of the song. You can automate anything you like, but try to put the song first and only do what's necessary. Most of the time it's likely that you won't have to automate all of the channels, or even all of the levels. I find that, once I've set up a static mix and sorted out the mutes, I don't usually need to automate more than around a third of the tracks that are playing, although of course a lot depends on the style of music with which I'm working.

When you think you've finished, listen carefully to the mix running under automation and, if possible, run off a copy on DAT, cassette or CD-R so that you can check the sound on other systems before going any further. You've saved the mix, so you can always come back to it later, but if you have an analogue mixer you should keep in mind that there are lots of mix controls that probably aren't automated (pan, EQ, aux sends and so on), not to mention any external effects and signal processors you might have patched in.

One useful trick is to use a pocket cassette recorder on which to keep notes about your mix. Before resetting your mixer you can then read the control settings of each mixer channel into the recorder. You can then go to the patchbay, make notes of any connections you have there, and finally you can record what outboard equipment is being used, what patches are being used, and – in the case of manual equipment – the control settings. When you next come to recreate the mix you can then play back the appropriate mini cassette and set up the controls as you've recorded them.

the benefits

Automated mixers don't make life easier or help you get the job done more quickly, but they do enable you to do a better job. Fine tuning a mix so that every little detail is taken care of is time consuming and requires a lot of concentration, and you'll probably find that the job takes you much longer than it did when you just ran the mix by hand.

If your studio is ever used by anyone other than yourself then automation becomes even more important, because it allows you to load up a mix you were working on months ago and carry on working with the confidence that the mixer settings are the same as they were when you left them. If you have a digital console and you're using only the built-in effects, you can recall the entire project and know that everything is just where you left it. Similarly, you can store your clients' projects so that, when they return after a few weeks to carry out the inevitable remix, you don't have to waste time in trying to recreate the original mix.

Using automation won't necessarily make you a better mix engineer, but it will allow you to become as good as you possibly can. At the very least it will allow you to hear what your mix sounds like in such a way that you don't have to split your concentration between listening and mixing. Snapshot or scene information is beneficial for even very simple static mixes, in that it can save or recall an entire mix at the press of a button or two. Digital automated mixers now cost little more than manually-operated analogue mixers did just a few years back, and it's probably fair to say that, in a few more years' time, it will be difficult to find a mixer that doesn't offer some form of automation.

common cable connections

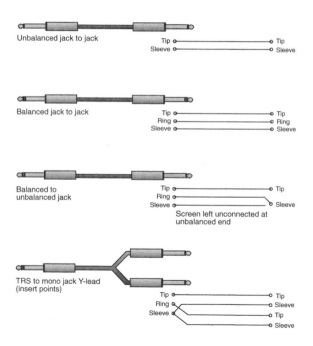

Unbalanced jack to jack

Tip o————————o Tip
Sleeve o————————o Sleeve

Balanced jack to jack

Tip o————————o Tip
Ring o————————o Ring
Sleeve o————————o Sleeve

Balanced to
unbalanced jack

Tip o————————o Tip
Ring o————————
Sleeve o————————o Sleeve

Screen left unconnected at
unbalanced end

TRS to mono jack Y-lead
(insert points)

Tip o————————o Tip
Ring o————————o Sleeve
Sleeve o————————o Tip
————————o Sleeve

125

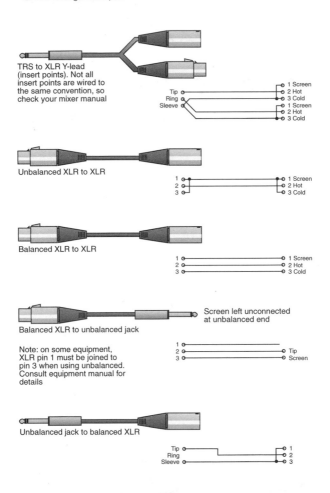

TRS to XLR Y-lead
(insert points). Not all
insert points are wired to
the same convention, so
check your mixer manual

Tip — 1 Screen
Ring — 2 Hot
Sleeve — 3 Cold
— 1 Screen
— 2 Hot
— 3 Cold

Unbalanced XLR to XLR

1 — 1 Screen
2 — 2 Hot
3 — 3 Cold

Balanced XLR to XLR

1 — 1 Screen
2 — 2 Hot
3 — 3 Cold

Balanced XLR to unbalanced jack

Screen left unconnected
at unbalanced end

Note: on some equipment,
XLR pin 1 must be joined to
pin 3 when using unbalanced.
Consult equipment manual for
details

1 —
2 — Tip
3 — Screen

Unbalanced jack to balanced XLR

Tip — 1
Ring — 2
Sleeve — 3

glossary

AC

Alternating Current.

active

Circuit containing transistors, ICs, tubes and other devices that require power to operate and are capable of amplification.

active sensing

System used to verify that a MIDI connection is working, in which the sending device frequently sends short messages to the receiving device to reassure it that all is well. If these active sensing messages stop for any reason, the receiving device will recognise a fault condition and switch off all notes. Not all MIDI devices support active sensing.

ADSR

Envelope generator with Attack, Decay, Sustain and Release parameters. This is a simple type of envelope generator and was first used on early analogue synthesisers, though similar envelopes may be found in some effects units to control filter sweeps and suchlike.

AFL

After-Fade Listen, a system used within mixing consoles to

allow specific signals to be monitored at the level set by their fader or level control knob. Aux sends are generally monitored AFL rather than PFL so that the actual signal being fed to an effects unit can be monitored.

aftertouch
Means of generating a control signal based on how much pressure is applied to the keys of a MIDI keyboard. Most instruments that support this do not have independent pressure sensing for all keys, but instead detect the overall pressure by means of a sensing strip running beneath the keys. Aftertouch may be used to control musical functions such as vibrato depth, filter brightness, loudness and so on, though it may also be used to control some parameter of a MIDI effects unit, such as delay feedback or effect level.

algorithm
Computer program designed to perform a specific task. In the context of effects units, algorithms usually describe a software building block designed to create a specific effect or combination of effects. All digital effects are based on algorithms.

ambience
The result of sound reflections in a confined space being added to the original sound. Ambience may also be created electronically by some digital reverb units. The main difference between ambience and reverberation is that ambience doesn't have the characteristic long delay time of reverberation – the reflections mainly give the sound a sense of space.

amp
Unit of electrical current, short for ampere.

amplifier
Device that increases the level of an electrical signal.

amplitude
Another word for level. Can refer to levels of sound or electrical signal.

analogue
Circuitry that uses a continually-changing voltage or current to represent a signal. The origin of the term is that the electrical signal can be thought of as being analogous to the original signal.

attack
Time taken for a sound to achieve maximum amplitude. Drums have a fast attack, whereas bowed strings have a slow attack. In compressors and gates, the attack time equates to how quickly the processor can change its gain.

attenuate
To make lower in level.

audio frequency
Signals in the human audio range, nominally 20Hz to 20kHz.

aux
Control on a mixing console designed to route a proportion of the channel signal to the effects or cue mix outputs (see Aux Send).

aux return
Mixer inputs used to add effects to the mix.

aux send

Physical output from a mixer aux send buss.

balance

This word has several meanings in recording. It may refer to the relative levels of the left and right channels of a stereo recording, or it may be used to describe the relative levels of the various instruments and voices within a mix.

bandpass filter (BDF)

Filter that removes or attenuates frequencies above and below the frequency at which it is set. Frequencies which fall within the waveband are emphasised. Bandpass filters are often used in synthesisers as tone-shaping elements.

bandwidth

Means of specifying the range of frequencies passed by an electronic circuit such as an amplifier, mixer or filter. The frequency range is usually measured at the points where the level drops by 3dB relative to the maximum.

binary

Counting system based on only two numbers: 1 and 0.

bit

Binary digit, which may either be 1 or 0.

boost/cut control

Single control which allows the range of frequencies passing through a filter to be either amplified or attenuated, according to the way in which it is set. The centre position is usually the 'flat' or 'no effect' position.

bouncing

Process of mixing two or more recorded tracks together and re-recording these onto another track.

BPM

Beats Per Minute.

buss

Common electrical signal path along which signals may travel. In a mixer, there are several busses carrying the stereo mix, the groups, the PFL signal, the aux sends and so on. Power supplies are also fed along busses.

byte

Piece of digital data comprising eight bits.

cardioid

Meaning heart shaped, describes the polar response of a unidirectional microphone.

channel

In the context of MIDI, Channel refers to one of 16 possible data channels over which MIDI data may be sent. The organisation of data by channels means that up to 16 different MIDI instruments or parts may be addressed using a single cable.

channel

In the context of mixing consoles, a channel is a single strip of controls relating to one input.

chase

Term describing the process whereby a slave device attempts to synchronise itself with a master device. In the context of a MIDI sequence, Chase may also involve chasing events – looking back to earlier positions in the song to see if there are any program changes or other events that need to be acted upon.

chip
Integrated circuit.

chord
Two or more different musical notes played at the same time.

chorus
Effect created by doubling a signal and adding delay and pitch modulation.

chromatic
Scale of pitches rising in steps of one semitone.

click track
Metronome pulse which helps musicians to keep time.

clipping
Severe form of distortion which occurs when a signal attempts to exceed the maximum level which a piece of equipment can handle.

common-mode rejection
Measure of how well a balanced circuit rejects a signal that is common to both inputs.

compander

Encode/decode device that compresses a signal while encoding it, then expands it when decoding it.

compressor

Device designed to reduce the dynamic range of audio signals by reducing the level of high signals or by increasing the level of low signals.

conductor

Material that provides a low resistance path for electrical current.

console

Alternative term for mixer.

crash

Slang term relating to malfunction of a computer program.

cut-and-paste editing

Copying or moving sections of a recording to different locations.

cutoff frequency

Frequency above or below which attenuation begins in a filter circuit.

cycle

One complete vibration of a sound source or its electrical equivalent. One cycle per second is expressed as one Hertz (Hz).

CV

Control Voltage. Used to control the pitch of an oscillator or filter frequency in an analogue synthesiser. Most analogue synthesisers follow a one volt per octave convention, though there are exceptions. To use a pre-MIDI analogue synthesiser under MIDI control, a MIDI-to-CV converter is required.

daisy chain
Term used to describe serial electrical connection between devices or modules.

damping
In the context of reverberation, damping refers to the rate at which reverberant energy is absorbed by the various surfaces in an environment.

DAT
Digital Audio Tape. The most commonly-used DAT machines are more correctly known as R-DATs because they use a rotating head similar to that in a video recorder. Digital recorders using fixed or stationary heads (such as DCC) are known as S-DAT machines.

data
Information stored and used by a computer.

data compression
System for reducing the amount of data stored by a digital system. Most audio data compression systems are known as lossy systems, as some of the original signal is discarded in accordance with psychoacoustic principles designed to ensure that only components which cannot be heard are lost.

dB
Decibel. Unit used to express the relative levels of two

electrical voltages, powers or sounds.

dBm
Variation on dB referenced to 0dB = 1mW into 600 ohms.

dBv
Variation on dB referenced to 0dB = 0.775v.

dBV
Variation on dB referenced to 0dB = 1V.

dB/octave
A means of measuring the slope of a filter. The more decibels per octave the sharper the filter slope.

dbx
A commercial encode/decode tape noise reduction system that compresses the signal during recording and expands it by an identical amount on playback.

DC
Direct Current.

DCC
Stationary-head digital recorder format developed by Philips. Uses a data-compression system to reduce the amount of data that needs to be stored.

DCO
Digitally-Controlled Oscillator.

DDL

Digital Delay Line.

decay
Progressive reduction in amplitude of a sound or electrical signal over time. In the context of an ADSR envelope shaper, the decay phase starts as soon as the attack phase has reached its maximum level. In the decay phase, the signal level drops until it reaches the sustain level set by the user. The signal then remains at this level until the key is released, at which point the release phase is entered.

de-esser
Device used to reduce the effect of sibilance present in vocal signals.

DI
Direct Inject, in which a signal is plugged directly into an audio chain without the aid of a microphone.

DI box
Device for matching the signal-level impedance of a source to a tape machine or mixer input.

digital
Electronic system which represents data and signals in the form of codes comprising 1s and 0s.

digital delay
Digital processor for generating delay and echo effects.

digital reverb
Digital processor for simulating reverberation.

DIN connector

Consumer multipin signal connection format, also used for MIDI cabling. Various pin configurations are available.

disc

Used to describe vinyl discs, CDs and MiniDiscs.

disk

Abbreviation of diskette, but now used to describe computer floppy, hard and removable disks (see Floppy Disk).

Dolby

An encode/decode tape noise reduction system that amplifies low-level, high-frequency signals during recording, then reverses this process during playback. There are several different Dolby systems in use, including types B, C and S for domestic and semi-professional machines, and types A and SR for professional machines. Recordings made whilst using one of these systems must also be replayed via the same system.

DOS

Disk Operating System. Part of the operating system of PC and PC-compatible computers.

driver

Piece of software that handles communications between the main program and a hardware peripheral, such as a soundcard, printer or scanner.

drum pad

Synthetic playing surface which produces electronic trigger

signals in response to being hit with drumsticks.

dry
Signal to which no effects have been added. Conversely, a sound which has been treated with an effect, such as reverberation, is referred to as wet.

DSP
Digital Signal Processor. A powerful microchip used to process digital signals.

dubbing
Adding further material to an existing recording. Also known as overdubbing.

ducking
System for controlling the level of one audio signal with another. For example, background music can be made to duck whenever there is a voice-over.

dump
To transfer digital data from one device to another. A Sysex dump is a means of transmitting information about a particular instrument or module over MIDI, and may be used to store sound patches, parameter settings and so on.

dynamic microphone
Type of microphone that works on the electric generator principle, whereby a diaphragm moves a coil of wire within a magnetic field.

dynamic range

Range in decibels between the highest signal that can be handled by a piece of equipment and the level at which small signals disappear into the noise floor.

dynamics
Method of describing the relative levels within a piece of music.

early reflections
First sound reflections from walls, floors and ceilings following a sound which is created in an acoustically reflective environment.

effects loop
Connection system that allows an external signal processor to be connected into the audio chain.

effects return
Additional mixer input designed to accommodate the output from an effects unit.

effects unit
Device for treating an audio signal in order to change it in some creative way. Effects often involve the use of delay circuits, and include such treatments as reverb and echo.

encode/decode
System that requires a signal to be processed prior to recording, which is then reversed during playback.

enhancer
Device designed to brighten audio material using techniques like dynamic equalisation, phase shifting and harmonic generation.

envelope

The way in which the level of a sound or signal varies over time.

envelope generator

Circuit capable of generating a control signal which represents the envelope of the sound you want to recreate. This may then be used to control the level of an oscillator or other sound source, though envelopes may also be used to control filter or modulation settings. The most common example is the ADSR generator.

E-PROM

Similar to ROM, but the information on the chip can be erased and replaced using special equipment.

equaliser

Device for selectively cutting or boosting selected parts of the audio spectrum.

erase

To remove recorded material from an analogue tape, or to remove digital data from any form of storage medium.

event

In MIDI terms, an event is a single unit of MIDI data, such as a note being turned on or off, a piece of controller information, a program change, and so on.

exciter

Enhancer that works by synthesising new high-frequency harmonics.

expander

Device designed to decrease the level of low-level signals and increase the level of high-level signals, thus increasing the dynamic range of the signal.

expander module

Synthesiser with no keyboard, often rack mountable or in some other compact format.

fader

Sliding potentiometer control used in mixers and other processors.

FET

Field Effect Transistor.

figure-of-eight

Describes the polar response of a microphone that is equally sensitive at both front and rear, yet rejects sounds coming from the sides.

file

Meaningful list of data stored in digitally. A Standard MIDI File is a specific type of file designed to allow sequence information to be exchanged between different types of sequencer.

filter

Electronic circuit designed to emphasise or attenuate a specific range of frequencies.

flanging

Modulated delay effect using feedback to create a dramatic,

sweeping sound.

floppy disk

Computer disk that uses a flexible magnetic medium encased in a protective plastic sleeve. The maximum capacity of a standard high-density disk is 1.44Mb. Earlier double-density disks hold only around half the amount of data.

flutter echo

Resonant echo that occurs when sound reflects back and forth between two parallel reflective surfaces.

foldback

System for feeding one or more separate mixes to the performers for use while recording and overdubbing. Also known as a cue mix.

format

Procedure required to make a computer disk ready to be used. The process of formatting organises the disk's surface into a series of electronic pigeonholes into which data can be stored. Different computers often use different formatting systems.

frequency

Indication of how many cycles of a repetitive waveform occur in one second. A waveform which has a repetition cycle of once per second has a frequency of 1Hz.

frequency response

Measurement of the frequency range that can be handled by a specific piece of electrical equipment or loudspeaker.

FSK
Frequency-Shift Keying. A method of recording a sync clock signal onto tape by representing it as two alternating tones.

fundamental
Any sound comprises a fundamental or basic frequency plus harmonics and partials at a higher frequency.

FX
Shorthand for effects.

gain
Amount by which a circuit amplifies a signal.

gate
Electrical signal generated whenever a key is depressed on an electronic keyboard. This is used to trigger envelope generators and other events that need to be synchronised to key action.

gate
Electronic device designed to mute low-level signals, thus improving the noise performance during pauses in the wanted material.

general MIDI
Addition to the basic MIDI spec to assure a minimum level of compatibility when playing back GM-format song files. The specification covers type and program, number of sounds, minimum levels of polyphony and multitimbrality, response to controller information and so on.

glitch

Describes an unwanted short-term corruption of a signal, or the unexplained short-term malfunction of a piece of equipment. For example, an inexplicable click on a DAT tape would be termed a glitch.

GM reset
Universal Sysex command which activates the General MIDI mode on a GM instrument. The same command also sets all controllers to their default values and switches off any notes still playing by means of an All Notes Off message.

graphic equaliser
Equaliser on which several narrow segments of the audio spectrum are controlled by individual cut/boost faders. The name derives from the fact that the fader positions provide a graphic representation of the EQ curve.

ground
Electrical earth, or zero volts. In mains wiring, the ground cable is physically connected to the ground via a long conductive metal spike.

ground loops
Also known as earth loops. Wiring problem in which currents circulate in the ground wiring of an audio system, known as the ground loop effect. When these currents are induced by the alternating mains supply, hum results.

group
Collection of signals within a mixer that are mixed and then routed through a separate fader to provide overall control. In a multitrack mixer, several groups are provided to feed the

various recorder track inputs.

GS
Roland's own extension to the General MIDI protocol.

hard disk
High-capacity computer storage device based on a rotating rigid disk with a magnetic coating onto which data may be recorded.

harmonic
High-frequency component of a complex waveform.

harmonic distortion
Addition of harmonics not present in the original signal.

head
Part of a tape machine or disk drive that reads and/or writes data to and from the storage media.

headroom
The safety margin in decibels between the highest peak signal being passed by a piece of equipment and the absolute maximum level the equipment can handle.

high-pass filter (HPF)
Filter which attenuates frequencies below its cutoff frequency.

hiss
Noise caused by random electrical fluctuations.

hum

Signal contamination caused by the addition of low frequencies, usually related to the mains power frequency.

Hz
Shorthand for Hertz, the unit of frequency.

IC
Integrated Circuit.

impedance
Can be visualised as the AC resistance of a circuit which contains both resistive and reactive components.

inductor
Reactive component which presents an impedance with increases with frequency.

initialise
To automatically restore a piece of equipment to its factory default settings.

insert point
Connector that allows an external processor to be patched into a signal path so that the signal then flows through the external processor.

insulator
Material that does not conduct electricity.

interface
Device that acts as an intermediary to two or more other pieces of equipment. For example, a MIDI interface enables a computer

to communicate with MIDI instruments and keyboards.

intermittent

Usually describes a fault that only appears occasionally.

intermodulation distortion

Form of distortion that introduces frequencies not present in the original signal. These are invariably based on the sum and difference products of the original frequencies.

I/O

The part of a system that handles inputs and outputs, usually in the digital domain.

IPS

Inches Per Second. Used to describe tape speed.

IRQ

Interrupt Request. Part of the operating system of a computer that allows a connected device to request attention from the processor in order to transfer data to it or from it.

isopropyl alcohol

Type of alcohol commonly used for cleaning and de-greasing tape machine heads and guides.

jack

Commonly used audio connector. May be mono (TS) or stereo (TRS).

jargon

Specialised words associated with a specialist subject.

k
Abbreviation for 1000 (kilo). Used as a prefix to other values to indicate magnitude.

kHz
1000Hz.

kohm
1000 ohms.

LCD
Liquid Crystal Display.

LED
Light-Emitting Diode. Solid-state lamp.

LSB
Least Significant Byte. If a piece of data has to be conveyed as two bytes, one byte represents high-value numbers and the other low-value numbers, in much the same way as tens and units function in the decimal system. The high value, or most significant part of the message, is called the Most Significant Byte or MSB.

limiter
Device that controls the gain of a signal so as to prevent it from ever exceeding a preset level. A limiter is essentially a fast-acting compressor with an infinite compression ratio.

line level
Mixers and signal processors tend to work at a standard signal level known as line level. In practice there are several different

standard line levels, but all are in the order of a few volts. A nominal signal level is around -10dBv for semi-pro equipment and +4dBv for professional equipment.

load
Electrical circuit that draws power from another circuit or power supply. Also describes reading data into a computer.

load on/off
Function to allow the keyboard and sound-generating section of a keyboard synthesiser to be used independently of each other.

logic
Type of electronic circuitry used for processing binary signals comprising two discrete voltage levels.

loop
Circuit where the output is connected back to the input.

low-frequency oscillator (LFO)
Oscillator used as a modulation source, usually below 20Hz. The most common LFO waveshape is the sine wave, though there is often a choice of sine, square, triangular and sawtooth waveforms.

low-pass filter (LPF)
A filter which attenuates frequencies above its cutoff frequency.

mA
Milliamp, or one thousandth of an amp.

MDM

Modular Digital Multitrack. A digital recorder that can be used in multiples to provide a greater number of synchronised tracks than a single machine.

meg

Abbreviation for 1,000,000.

memory

Computer's RAM memory used to store programs and data. This data is lost when the computer is switched off and so must be stored to disk or other suitable media.

mic level

Low-level signal generated by a microphone. This must be amplified many times to increase it to line level.

microprocessor

Specialised microchip at the heart of a computer. It is here that instructions are read and acted upon.

MIDI

Musical Instrument Digital Interface.

MIDI analyser

Device that gives a visual readout of MIDI activity when connected between two pieces of MIDI equipment.

MIDI bank change

Type of controller message used to select alternate banks of MIDI programs where access to more than 128 programs is required.

MIDI controller

Term used to describe the physical interface by means of which the musician plays the MIDI synthesiser or other sound generator. Examples of controllers are keyboards, drum pads, wind synths and so on.

MIDI control change

Also known as MIDI Controllers or Controller Data. These messages convey positional information relating to performance controls such as wheels, pedals, switches and other devices. This information can be used to control functions such as vibrato depth, brightness, portamento, effects levels, and many other parameters.

(standard) MIDI file

Standard file format for storing song data recorded on a MIDI sequencer in such as way as to allow it to be read by other makes or models of MIDI sequencer.

MIDI implementation chart

A chart, usually found in MIDI product manuals, which provides information as to which MIDI features are supported. Supported features are marked with a 0 while unsupported feature are marked with a X. Additional information may be provided, such as the exact form of the bank change message.

MIDI in

The socket used to receive information from a master controller or from the MIDI Thru socket of a slave unit.

MIDI merge

Device or sequencer function that enables two or more

streams of MIDI data to be combined.

MIDI mode

MIDI information can be interpreted by the receiving MIDI instrument in a number of ways, the most common being polyphonically on a single MIDI channel (poly-omni off mode). Omni mode enables a MIDI Instrument to play all incoming data regardless of channel.

MIDI module

Sound-generating device with no integral keyboard.

MIDI note number

Every key on a MIDI keyboard has its own note number, ranging from 0 to 127, where 60 represents middle C. Some systems use C3 as middle C while others use C4.

MIDI note off

MIDI message sent when key is released.

MIDI note on

Message sent when note is pressed.

MIDI out

MIDI connector used to send data from a master device to the MIDI In of a connected slave device.

MIDI port

MIDI connections of a MIDI-compatible device. A multiport, in the context of a MIDI interface, is a device with multiple MIDI output sockets, each capable of carrying data relating to a different set of 16 MIDI channels. Multiports are the only means of exceeding the limitations imposed by 16 MIDI channels.

MIDI program change
Type of MIDI message used to change sound patches on a remote module or the effects patch on a MIDI effects unit.

MIDI splitter
Alternative term for MIDI thru box.

MIDI sync
Description of the synchronisation systems available to MIDI users: MIDI Clock and MIDI Time Code.

MIDI thru
Socket on a slave unit used to feed the MIDI In socket of the next unit in line.

MIDI thru box
Device which splits the MIDI Out signal of a master instrument or sequencer to avoid daisy chaining. Powered circuitry is used to 'buffer' the outputs so as to prevent problems when many pieces of equipment are driven from a single MIDI output.

mixer
Device for combining two or more audio signals.

monitor
Reference loudspeaker used for mixing.

monitor
VDU for a computer.

monitoring
Action of listening to a mix or a specific audio signal.

monophonic
One note at a time.

motherboard
Main circuit board within a computer into which all the other components plug or connect.

MTC
MIDI Time Code. A MIDI sync implementation based on SMPTE time code.

multisample
Creation of several samples, each covering a limited musical range, the idea being to produce a more natural range of sounds across the range of the instrument being sampled. For example, a piano may need to be sampled every two or three semitones in order to sound convincing.

multitimbral module
MIDI sound source capable of producing several different sounds at the same time and controlled on different MIDI channels.

multitrack
Recording device capable of recording several 'parallel' parts or tracks which may then be mixed or re-recorded independently.

near field

Some people prefer the term 'close field' to describe a loudspeaker system designed to be used close to the listener. The advantage is that the listener hears more of the direct sound from the speakers and less of the reflected sound from the room.

noise reduction
System for reducing analogue tape noise or for reducing the level of hiss present in a recording.

noise shaping
System for creating digital dither so that any added noise is shifted into those parts of the audio spectrum where the human ear is least sensitive.

non-linear recording
Describes digital recording systems that allow any parts of the recording to be played back in any order with no gaps. Conventional tape is referred to as linear, because the material can only play back in the order in which it was recorded.

non-registered parameter number
Addition to the basic MIDI spec that allows controllers 98 and 99 to be used to control non-standard parameters relating to particular models of synthesiser. This is an alternative to using system-exclusive data to achieve the same ends, though NRPNs tend to be used mainly by Yamaha and Roland instruments.

normalise
A socket is said to be normalised when it is wired such that the original signal path is maintained, unless a plug is inserted into the socket. The most common examples of normalised

connectors are the insert points on a mixing console.

nut
Slotted plastic or bone component at the headstock end of a guitar neck used to guide the strings over the fingerboard, and to space the strings above the frets.

Nyquist theorem
The rule which states that a digital sampling system must have a sample rate at least twice as high as that of the highest frequency being sampled in order to avoid aliasing. Because anti-aliasing filters aren't perfect, the sampling frequency usually has to be made more than twice that of the maximum input frequency.

octave
When a frequency or pitch is transposed up by one octave, its frequency is doubled.

off-line
Process carried out while a recording is not playing. For example, some computer-based processes have to be carried out off-line as the computer isn't fast enough to carry out the process in real time.

ohm
Unit of electrical resistance.

omni
Refers to a microphone that is equally sensitive in all directions, or to the MIDI mode in which data on all channels is recognised.

open circuit
Break in an electrical circuit that prevents current from flowing.

open reel
Tape machine on which the tape is wound on spools rather than sealed in a cassette.

operating system
Basic software that enables a computer to load and run other programs.

opto-electronic device
Device on which some electrical parameters change in response to a variation in light intensity. Variable photoresistors are sometimes used as gain control elements in compressors where the side-chain signal modulates the light intensity.

oscillator
Circuit designed to generate a periodic electrical waveform.

overdub
To add another part to a multitrack recording or to replace one of the existing parts.

overload
To exceed the operating capacity of an electronic or electrical circuit.

pad
Resistive circuit for reducing signal level.

pan pot
Control enabling the user of a mixer to move the signal to any point in the stereo soundstage by varying the relative levels fed to the left and right stereo outputs.

parallel
Method of connecting two or more circuits together so that their inputs and outputs are all connected together.

parameter
Variable value that affects some aspect of a device's performance.

parametric EQ
Equaliser with separate controls for frequency, bandwidth and cut/boost.

passive
Circuit with no active elements.

patch
Alternative term for program. Referring to a single programmed sound within a synthesiser that can be called up using program-change commands. MIDI effects units and samplers also have patches.

patch bay
System of panel-mounted connectors used to bring inputs and outputs to a central point from where they can be routed using plug-in patch cords.

patch cord
Short cable used with patch bays.

peak

Maximum instantaneous level of a signal.

peak

The highest signal level in any section of programme material.

PFL

Pre-Fade Listen. A system used within a mixing console to allow the operator to listen in on a selected signal, regardless of the position of the fader controlling that signal.

phantom power

48V DC supply for capacitor microphones, transmitted along the signal cores of a balanced mic cable.

phase

Timing difference between two electrical waveforms expressed in degrees where 360° corresponds to a delay of exactly one cycle.

phaser

Effect which combines a signal with a phase-shifted version of itself to produce creative filtering effects. Most phasers are controlled by means of an LFO.

phono plug

Hi-fi connector developed by RCA and used extensively on semi-pro, unbalanced recording equipment.

pickup

The part of a guitar that converts string vibrations into

electrical signals.

pitch
Musical interpretation of an audio frequency.

pitch bend
Special control message specifically designed to produce a change in pitch in response to the movement of a pitch bend wheel or lever. Pitch bend data can be recorded and edited, just like any other MIDI controller data, even though it isn't part of the controller message group.

pitch shifter
Device for changing the pitch of an audio signal without changing its duration.

polyphony
An instrument's ability to play two or more notes simultaneously. An instrument which can play only one note at a time is described as monophonic.

poly mode
The most common MIDI mode, which allows any instrument to respond to multiple simultaneous notes transmitted on a single MIDI channel.

port
Connection for the input or output of data.

portamento
Gliding effect that allows a sound to change pitch at a gradual rate rather than abruptly when a new key is pressed or MIDI

note sent.

post-production

Work done to a stereo recording after mixing is complete.

post-fade

Aux signal taken from after the channel fader so that the aux send level follows any channel fader changes. Normally used for feeding effects devices.

power supply

Unit designed to convert mains electricity to the voltages necessary to power an electronic circuit or device.

PPM

Peak Programme Meter. A meter designed to register signal peaks rather than the average level.

PPQN

Pulsed Per Quarter Note. Used in the context of MIDI clock-derived sync signals.

PQ coding

Process for adding pause, cue and other subcode information to a digital master tape in preparation for CD manufacture.

pre-emphasis

System for applying high-frequency boost to a sound before processing so as to reduce the effect of noise. A corresponding de-emphasis process is required on playback so as to restore the original signal and to attenuate any high-frequency noise contributed by the recording process.

pre-fade

Aux signal taken from before the channel fader so that the channel fader has no effect on the aux send level. Normally used for creating foldback or cue mixes.

preset

Effects unit or synth patch that cannot be altered by the user.

pressure

Alternative term for aftertouch.

print through

Undesirable process that causes some magnetic information from a recorded analogue tape to become imprinted onto an adjacent layer. This can produce low-level pre- or post-echoes.

processor

Device designed to treat an audio signal by changing its dynamics or frequency content. Examples of processors include compressors, gates and equalisers.

program change

MIDI message designed to change instrument or effects unit patches.

pulse wave

Similar to a square wave but non-symmetrical. Pulse waves sound brighter and thinner than square waves, making them useful in the synthesis of reed instruments. The timbre changes according to the mark/space ratio of the waveform.

pulse-width modulation

Means of modulating the duty cycle (mark/space ratio) of a pulse wave. This changes the timbre of the basic tone. LFO modulation of pulse width can be used to produce a pseudo-chorus effect.

punch-in
Action of placing an already recorded track into record at the correct time during playback so that the existing material may be extended or replaced.

punch-out
Action of switching a tape machine (or other recording device) out of record after executing a punch in. With most multitrack machines, both punching in and punching out can be accomplished without stopping the tape.

PZM
Pressure Zone Microphone. A type of boundary microphone, designed to reject out-of-phase sounds reflected from surfaces within the recording environment.

Q
Measurement of the resonant properties of a filter. The higher the Q, the more resonant the filter and the narrower the range of frequencies that are allowed to pass.

quantising
Means of moving notes recorded in a MIDI sequencer so that they line up with user defined subdivisions of a musical bar – 16s, for example. The facility may be used to correct timing errors, but over-quantising can remove the human feel from a performance.

RAM

Abbreviation for Random Access Memory. This is a type of memory used by computers for the temporary storage of programs and data, and all data is lost when the power is turned off. For that reason, work needs to be saved to disk if it is not to be lost.

R-DAT

Digital tape machine using a rotating head system.

real time

Audio process that can be carried out as the signal is being recorded or played back. The opposite is off-line, where the signal is processed in non-real time.

release

Time taken for a level or gain to return to normal. Often used to describe the rate at which a synthesised sound reduces in level after a key has been released.

resistance

Opposition to the flow of electrical current. Measured in ohms.

resolution

Accuracy with which an analogue signal is represented by a digitising system. The more bits are used, the more accurately the amplitude of each sample can be measured, but there are other elements of converter design that also affect accuracy. High conversion accuracy is known as high resolution.

resonance

Same as Q.

reverb

Acoustic ambience created by multiple reflections in a confined space.

RF

Radio Frequency.

RF interference

Interference significantly above the range of human hearing.

ribbon microphone

Microphone in which the sound-capturing element is a thin metal ribbon suspended in a magnetic filed. When sound causes the ribbon to vibrate, a small electrical current is generated within the ribbon.

ring modulator

Device that accepts and processes two input signals in a particular way. The output signal does not contain any of the original input signal but instead comprises new frequencies based on the sum and difference of the input signal's frequency components. The best-known application of ring modulation is the creation of Dalek voices, but it may also be used to create dramatic instrumental textures. Depending on the relationships between the input signals, the results may either be musical or extremely dissonant – for example, ring modulation can be used to create bell-like tones. (The term 'ring' is used because the original circuit which produced the effect used a ring of diodes.)

RMS

Root Mean Square. A method of specifying the behaviour of a

piece of electrical equipment under continuous sine wave testing conditions.

roll-off
The rate at which a filter attenuates a signal once it has passed the filter cutoff point.

ROM
Abbreviation for Read-Only Memory. This is a permanent and non-volatile type of memory containing data that can't be changed. Operating systems are often stored on ROM as the memory remains intact when the power is switched off.

safety copy
Copy or clone of an original tape for use in case of loss of or damage to the original.

sample
Process carried out by an A/D converter where the instantaneous amplitude of a signal is measured many times per second (44.1kHz in the case of CD).

sample
Digitised sound used as a musical sound source in a sampler or additive synthesiser.

sample and hold
Usually refers to a feature whereby random values are generated at regular intervals and then used to control another function such as pitch or filter frequency. Sample and hold circuits were also used in old analogue synthesisers to 'remember' the note being played after a key had been released.

sample rate

Number of times which an A/D converter samples the incoming waveform each second.

sawtooth wave

So called because it resembles the teeth of a saw, this waveform contains only even harmonics.

SCSI

(Pronounced 'skuzzi'.) Small Computer System Interface. An interfacing system for using hard drives, scanners, CD-ROM drives and similar peripherals with a computer. Each SCSI device has its own ID number and no two SCSI devices in the same chain must be set to the same number. The last SCSI device in the chain should be terminated either via an internal terminator, where provided, or via a plug-in terminator fitted to a free SCSI socket.

sequencer

Device for recording and replaying MIDI data, usually in a multitrack format, allowing complex compositions to be built up a part at a time.

short circuit

Low-resistance path that allows electrical current to flow. The term is usually used to describe a current path that exists through a faulty condition.

sibilance

High-frequency whistling or lisping sound that affects vocal recordings due either to poor mic technique or excessive equalisation.

side chain
Part of a circuit that splits off a proportion of the main signal to be processed in some way. Compressors use a side-chain signal to derive their control signals.

signal
Electrical representation of input such as sound.

signal chain
Route taken by a signal from the input of a system to its output.

signal-to-noise ratio
Ratio of maximum signal level to the residual noise, expressed in decibels.

sine wave
Waveform of a pure tone with no harmonics.

single-ended noise reduction
Device for removing or attenuating the noise component of a signal. Doesn't require previous coding, as in the case of Dolby or dbx.

slave
Device under the control of a master device.

SMPTE
Time code developed for the film industry but now extensively used in music and recording. SMPTE is a real-time code and is related to hours, minutes, seconds and film or video frames rather than to musical tempo.

SPL
Sound-Pressure Level. Measured in decibels.

SPP
Song-Position Pointer (MIDI).

standard MIDI file
Standard file format that allows MIDI files to be transferred between different sequencers and MIDI file players.

step time
System for programming a sequencer in non-real time.

stereo
Two-channel system feeding left and right loudspeakers.

stripe
To record time code onto one track of a multitrack tape machine.

square wave
Symmetrical rectangular waveform. Square waves contain a series of odd harmonics.

sub-bass
Frequencies below the range of typical monitor loudspeakers. Some define sub-bass as frequencies that can be felt rather than heard.

subcode
Hidden data within the CD and DAT format that includes such information as the absolute time location, number of tracks, total running time and so on.

subtractive synthesis

Process of creating a new sound by filtering and shaping a raw, harmonically complex waveform.

surge

Sudden increase in mains voltage.

sustain

Part of the ADSR envelope which determines the level to which the sound will settle if a key is held down. Once the key is released, the sound decays at a rate set by the release parameter. Also refers to a guitar's ability to hold notes which decay very slowly.

sweet spot

Optimum position for a microphone or a listener relative to monitor loudspeakers.

switching power supply

Type of power supply that uses a high-frequency oscillator prior to the transformer in order that a smaller, lighter transformer may be used. These power supplies are commonly used in computers and some synthesiser modules.

sync

System for making two or more pieces of equipment run in synchronism with each other.

synthesiser

Electronic musical instrument designed to create a wide range of sounds, both imitative and abstract.

tape head

Part of a tape machine that transfers magnetic energy to the tape during recording or reads it during playback.

tempo

Rate of the beat of a piece of music, measured here in beats per minute.

test tone

Steady, fixed-level tone recorded onto a multitrack or stereo recording to act as a reference when matching levels.

THD

Total Harmonic Distortion.

thru

MIDI connector which passes on the signal received at the MIDI In socket.

timbre

Tonal 'colour' of a sound.

track

This term dates back to multitrack tape, on which the tracks are physical stripes of recorded material located side by side along the length of the tape.

tracking

System whereby one device follows another. Tracking is often discussed in the context of MIDI guitar synthesisers or controllers where the MIDI output attempts to track the pitch of the guitar strings.

transducer

Device for converting one form of energy into another. A microphone is a good example of a transducer, as it converts mechanical energy to electrical energy.

transparency

Subjective term used to describe audio quality where the high-frequency detail is clear and individual sounds are easy to identify and separate.

transpose

To shift a musical signal by a fixed number of semitones.

tremolo

Modulation of the amplitude of a sound using an LFO.

triangle wave

Symmetrical, triangle-shaped wave containing only odd harmonics, but with a lower harmonic content than the square wave.

TRS jack

Stereo-type jack with tip, ring and sleeve connections.

unbalanced

Two-wire electrical signal connection where the inner (hot or positive) conductor is usually surrounded by the cold (negative) conductor, forming a screen against interference.

unison

To play the same melody using two or more different instruments or voices.

valve
Vacuum-tube amplification component, also known as a tube.

velocity
The rate at which a key is depressed. This may be used to control loudness (to simulate the response of instruments such as pianos) or other parameters on later synthesisers.

vibrato
Pitch modulation using an LFO to modulate a VCO.

vocoder
Signal processor that imposes a changing spectral filter on a sound based on the frequency characteristics of a second sound. By taking the spectral content of a human voice and imposing it on a musical instrument, talking instrument effects can be created.

voice
Capacity of a synthesiser to play a single musical note. An instrument capable of playing 16 simultaneous notes is said to be a 16-voice instrument.

volt
Unit of electrical power.

VU meter
Meter designed to interpret signal levels in roughly the same way as the human ear, which responds more closely to the average levels of sounds rather than to the peak levels.

wah pedal

Guitar effects device where a bandpass filter is varied in frequency by means of a pedal control.

warmth
Subjective term used to describe sound where the bass and low mid frequencies have depth and where the high frequencies are smooth sounding rather than being aggressive or fatiguing. Warm-sounding tube equipment may also exhibit some of the aspects of compression.

watt
Unit of electrical power.

waveform
Graphic representation of the way in which a sound wave or electrical wave varies with time.

white noise
Random signal with an energy distribution that produces the same amount of noise power per Hz.

write
To save data to a digital storage medium, such as a hard drive.

XG
Yamaha's alternative to Roland's GS system for enhancing the General MIDI protocol so as to provide additional banks of patches and further editing facilities.

XLR
Type of connector commonly used to carry balanced audio signals, including the feeds from microphones.

Y-lead

Lead split so that one source can feed two destinations. Y-leads may also be used in console insert points, when a stereo jack plug at one end of the lead is split into two monos at the other.

zero crossing point

Point at which a signal waveform crosses from being positive to negative and vice versa.

zipper noise

Audible steps that occur when a parameter is being varied in a digital audio processor.